Living Death

Janis Tait

Living Death

Janis Tait

Indra Publishing

Indra Publishing
PO Box 7, Briar Hill, Victoria, 3088, Australia

© Janis Tait 2005
Typeset in Palatino by Midland Typesetters, Australia
Pre-press by The Image Company
Made and Printed in Australia by Centre State Printing

National Library of Australia
Cataloguing-in-Publication data:

    Tait, Janis, 1950– .
    Living death.

    ISBN 1 920787 14 3.

    1. Tait, Janis, 1950– . 2. Suicide – Psychological aspects.
    3. Bereavement – Psychological aspects. 4. Suicide
    victims – Family relationships. I. Title.

362.283

Contents

If, like the apricot tree
You'd been able to fully mature
You wouldn't have missed out on
Listening to Acker Bilk on the scratched LP
I found at a garage sale

Not that you'd appreciate old Acker
Still, you'd listen
How else would you know
The difference between 'cool' and 'uncool'.

Just like having had you
I'm able to know the difference
Between 'good' and 'bad' love

Chapter 1

––

I surface from a deep sleep to the phone screeching. It's the middle of the night. 'Yes, what's wrong?' I say.

'I've found this note on the table.' It's my eldest son's grandmother. Her frantic voice clutches at my throat.

'Read it to me.' All I hear are the words, 'So sorry. So very, very sorry'.

'The note was under his wallet,' she says.

A memory flashes of the time my friend left her wedding and engagement rings and wallet on the kitchen table before she went to end her life.

'I'm hanging up to ring the police,' I tell her.

In my red pyjamas with the teddy-bear motif, I hit 000. My husband watches, his eyes registering fear.

I tell the calm voice on the other end of the line, 'My son has left a suicide note. No, he has never done this before. Never ever threatened to take his life. Yes, he has been sick, but he's better now. He means it. I know he means it.'

I give the address where he lives with his grandmother. The clock shows only three minutes have passed since the alarm call. The operator says something supportive, but I don't take it in.

The phone's in the cradle. I'm in bed. I want my son back in his cradle where I could rock him and keep him safe.

My feet are on the floor. I'm putting on the dressing gown. Fleeing to the kitchen that's at the other end of the house, away from the bedrooms of my two younger sons. Already I am trying to protect them from what is about to happen.

1

Husband follows me. Sits at the table, stunned. I boil the kettle. Put too much milk in the tea. Light a cigarette. Smoke it beneath the exhaust fan. Pace from the fridge to the phone to the exhaust fan. I don't drink the tea. Ten minutes pass. We say nothing. We wait. I imagine my son sitting on a railway track waiting for the first train. The police will save him. He must mean it. He's never talked about suicide to me. Never, in all he's been through, has he wanted to put an end to it. I grab the phone on the first ring. A stranger, Constable something. Someone else who says, 'He's so sorry, so very sorry'.

Beneath the fluorescent light that holds three dead moths, I hear my beautiful son is dead. Found in the backyard. Could I come over and identify his body?

I could've been in the local fruit shop. The fruiterer saying, sorry, we're all out of pineapples. Sold out. Come back later today. Instead, I learned my son had sold out on life.

'He's dead. He's dead!' I scream at my husband, but the words come out in a strangled whisper.

I'm running down the long hallway when I'm back in the dream that's plagued me forever. Running as fast as I can, yet never moving, as the stranger in black approaches.

I knock into the walls as I run around the bedroom. What do I do? Light. I need light. I grab the cord of the drapes. Yank it so hard it leaves a rope burn on my hand. Get dressed. Just get dressed. 'What do I wear, what do I wear?' I ask the line of clothes that hang so straight. I yank them from their hangers, throw them in the air. They land on the bed. An unruly patchwork of colours. I hiss-scream at my husband who's behind me each step I take, 'What will I wear?'

'I don't know,' he says, 'anything,' sobs catching in his voice. As if I can't decide what to wear to a dance! Never again, I vow, will I wonder what to wear.

Somehow I'm dressed. Husband says he's coming too. 'No', I say, 'the boys might wake. And when they do one of us must be

2

here to tell them.' The cord burn stings even more as I wring my hands. 'No, you stay here. I'll go. Tell the boys nothing. I'll be home before they get up.'

Dawn breaking. Heart frozen. Body melting with tears. I put the windscreen wipers on, but it's my tears that stop me from seeing. Red light. People stare. I light a cigarette. Fuck him. He can't say anything this time about me smoking in the car. I light another and another. My jumper is wet from snot.

I bend to open the rusted gate. Am still bent as I walk the path, avoiding all the cracks, for I don't want to break my dead mother's back. An arm at my elbow; I'm being led to the front door.

'Where's my son?'

'Come in through the front way,' says the man too young to be investigating death. He tries to steer me into the house. I wrench free. Walk past rotting palings. In the far corner of the backyard a small group huddles over a covered form. Again the policeman tries to steer me inside. I elbow away his concern. Beside the draped form is a bottlebrush, its branches bent from your weight. Branches festooned with knotted material. Branches that point to the brick edging skewed from your final mid-air steps.

Now I welcome the hand on my elbow that leads me to the kitchen. On the table your final words, wallet empty of money. Nanna in the sagging chair. I hold her to me, head wedged between my breasts.

'How could he do this to me!' she wails.

My words have disappeared.

'Have you got a minute?' asks the man whose clothes are blue and white. 'We need you to identify him now.' He opens the front door and I see parked in the driveway a station wagon with tinted windows. The tailgate is down. What looks to be a white parcel sticking out the end. Someone slides the parcel out further.

You've lost so much weight and the line around your neck is

so thin and your right eye is half open, winking at me as if it's all a joke. Cold, so very cold. The moment I touch you, I know you have already gone to another place. What I hold is just a mother-of-pearl shell. I sit on the tailgate and gather the shell that was you to me. Rock you and me; tell you and me it'll be all right. How much you must have been hurting. Why didn't you wait for me? I say other things like, 'what a duffer you are', silly things that you say to your children when they fall over and split their skin. I kiss the closed eye.

'This is your son?'

'Yes. My beautiful son.' I pull the sheet tight around you. 'Close the door. Keep him warm,' I say as I climb off the tailgate. Though dark windows conceal you, I still see your blue tongue. A bruise on the yellow sun rising.

In what should be the dining room, but which houses only two chairs covered with faded pansies and a telephone table with vinyl seat, I stand in the middle of the room, hands clasped as if holding myself together. Mentally I begin writing the script for the performance that must now be carried out.

Your father. I must ring him immediately. His home phone rings out. Though it's too early for him to be at work, Nanna gives me his work number. It's the wrong number. I never realised a telephone book had so many pages, was so heavy. Finally, the number of his workplace. 'Urgent,' I tell the girl who takes the message. 'Tell him it's urgent.' I imagine he will think the urgency's about his mother. Imagine he will be relieved it's only his son. His only son.

A grey-haired, short woman, carrying a black case comes into the room. She shakes my hand, tells me she's the coroner. I find myself thanking her profusely like she's done me the biggest favour. I haven't a clue what, though. I guess I'm hoping she was gentle with my son.

'I can't imagine what you must be feeling,' she says. It seems so natural when she puts her arms around me. Two mothers. One

4

dreading and one in the midst of dread. 'I have a son the same age as yours,' she whispers. She has a mint breath. To kill the taste of death, I suppose. She places a pamphlet in my hand. Apologises for not being able to spend more time with me, but she's got quite a few calls to make. The film, *Death Takes a Holiday*, comes to mind. This will happen many times over the next months. Crazy thoughts and images will continue to flash as my mind short-circuits from the overload.

I stand on the porch and watch as the driver slowly takes you down the narrow driveway, past the rusted gate, and turns left. So many times I've stood on a porch waving you off. The coroner has quietly slipped away too. Inside the police have finished taking notes. Are they satisfied of no foul play? (Though hanging must be the foulest play of all.) They tell me that I will need to go to my local police station to make a statement, and that your friends and family, even Nanna will need to make a statement.

'That girlfriend of his, says Nanna, 'when you interview her, tell her she's not to come to the funeral. We don't want her there. She's the cause of all this!'

Nanna and I are left sitting in the room that has chipped ducks on the wall flying to nowhere. I answer the phone, glad of something to do. I tell my first husband his son is dead. I say nothing then, listening for a sign, something to show he really cared. It's me that breaks the silence, as I tell him to hurry over to his mother as I must get home to my other sons.

As I'm leaving, Nanna says: 'He tidied up first. Wiped the ashtray clean. Put the brandy bottle in the rubbish bin outside.'

Most people with your illness lose their sense of pride and tend to become unkempt, slovenly. Not you. Always your hygiene and demeanor were spot on.

'You know,' she continues, 'last night he told me he'd be sitting up for a while, that he couldn't sleep. I got up to go to the toilet at about one o'clock. Saw the light on in the lounge, but didn't

5

think anything of it, seeing he was staying up late. If only I'd looked in then, perhaps...'

I kiss her 'if onlys' silent. There will be plenty of time for them later.

Driving home I pass commuters hurrying to work while I hurry from death. Numbness pervades me. Too soon the insidious taste and smell of death will inhabit me forever. I am on cruise control, stopping at red lights, giving way to pedestrians, driving at the legal speed. I squeeze my eyes, try to force the tears. I have frozen and will never thaw. My time in the army taught me that when under attack, the body will do one of three things: Freeze, flee, retaliate. Already I look forward to the second stage.

Up Bell Street, past my favourite greenery that has a flapping purple and white banner boasting, 'Nursery of the Year', towards the Yarra River. As I go over the bridge, I yearn to embrace you. Frantically I search through the slideshow stored behind my hazel eyes, finger my heart, reach into my gut. Everything's inaccessible behind the door of ice.

I gulp deep breaths; force myself to feel something, anything. I think of my father. How in his day he had to wind up the gramophone, whereas now we slot in a disc. And of my mother. How in her day she wore rags between her legs and now an assembly line spits out sanitised plugs. And in my day how death was like a fiction. Unlike today.

For all I know I could have driven to the moon and back, yet somehow I'm pulling into the brick driveway that's edged with leaning daffodils. Strange, I lock the car when the most valuable thing has already been stolen from me. The newspaper again has landed in the lavender bush. Last week I rang the news agency and said, tongue-in-cheek, that I hoped they had public liability for I'd be taking action if my lavender continued to be damaged by the careless paperboy. How ludicrous it all is. There was I distraught over the lopping of my lavender bush, when you were distraught over life. The paper falls open at headlines of war raging in the Middle East and of a suicide bomber. You barracked for the Bombers too.

No matter the season, always the outside awning is pulled down over the study window. To protect the computer my husband says. I stand there staring at the striped awning that today makes the house look as though it's winking at me. Like you just did.

The cats circle my feet. Their loud miaows encroach on the stillness. The responsibility for feeding them seems such a huge one. 'In a minute!' I tell them, ashamed at how ordinary my voice sounds. Surely, at the very least, a tremble, a tremor, a high note in honour of the dead.

The sun shines on my husband who sits as though he has no stuffing. He comes to me, wraps his long arms around me. I cannot lift mine for they are too heavy.

'There are things we have to do,' I say, trying hard to think what is next in the unwritten script. But all I can think about is this thing I'm feeling. A hollowness that will never be filled. I need to garner strength to tell my boys who still sleep. I hear a clicking and realise my husband is stirring sugar in the cup of tea before me, though I never take sugar. 'What do you become when you lose a son?' I say.

'You don't change,' he says.

I shrug his hand from my shoulder. 'You must!'

He sighs, but it's as if he's got nothing left to exhale. 'Why must you?'

'If you lose things like a purse, you become broke, you lose a husband, you become a widow…and…' Frantically I try to grab at, to label, another sort of loss.

'You will always be his mother.' He is crying. I hate him for being able to so easily purge his grief.

'If you lose your parents you become an orphan!'

'Mother. You are his mother. Always and forever.' He cradles his face in his arms and sobs as I've never heard him. I want to reach out and touch him but I have this heightened awareness of saving my energy for carrying my boys through the next few weeks.

When he has quietened, I give him a hanky and tell him it's time to tell the boys.

Middle son sleeps spread-eagled on his stomach. Such a sound sleeper, yet when my fingers barely touch his back he's immediately awake, eyes squinting in confusion. What ugliness is showing on my face, for he instantly knows before I utter a word?

'No! Oh Mum, no. No!'

I gather him to me, this nineteen-year-old who, till this moment, had no idea of how hideous pain could be.

'How?' he whispers.

'He hung himself, Darling. He hung himself.' As I say these words, even though I've touched the mark scored around your neck, seen your blue tongue swollen, it's like I'm an observer reporting a catastrophe in a country so foreign to me.

'Oh, fuck, Mum. I knew this would eventually happen,' he says, brown eyes already registering the impact.

'We must wake your brother.'

Like playing at Santa, the three of us creep in the blue and red and yellow bedroom. I sit on the bed. My husband shadows us as he relies on me to do the telling. 'Wake up,' I whisper, to my youngest son, the one who was closest to you. 'C'mon, wake up.' I rub his shoulder. 'We need to…'

'Get out,' he mumbles, burrowing beneath the doona. 'Let me sleep.'

'You must wake up, Darling.'

'What?' He peers from beneath titian eyelashes. Sees the unusual gathering. Sits bolt upright. 'What is it!'

'It's your brother. I'm so sorry to have to tell you this.' His blue eyes pierce mine as if pleading me to hold my tongue. 'He died during the night.'

I, me the observer, watch as my youngest tries to absorb the simple words that have spilled blood. He says nothing. Turns away from the sight of me, the messenger who brings news no brother should have to hear. Then that sound that comes from the deepest part of him; a lamentation of the sort I will never hear again.

'Leave me alone,' he manages to say, his face turned to the wall.

My husband is loath to leave him, but I push him out the door. I lead my middle son to his bedroom, lower him to the bed, and pull the doona up to his neck. Tell him to lie there, just for a while. Tell him that I'll ring the university. That he won't be sitting his exams. He nods, allowing me to do everything, anything, that will cancel the reality, at the very least, make it all seem bearable.

So many calls to make. Who to ring first? In order of seniority, blood-lines, emotional attachment? The secretary in me begins formulating mental lists of the most organised people who, when told of the calamity, will automatically ring another four people who will then ring others. A verbal chain letter of the most miserable proportions and one that will ultimately only bring a reward of sandwiches and tea and whatever people bring to the wake.

Still my youngest son makes the woeful sound. I know to leave him alone for the moment, for he will better regain his equilibrium, as wobbly as it will be.

Selfishly, I ring two of my brothers first for they will come immediately. Theirs are the hugs I need now. The hugs we never gave each other as children but that are plentiful now we're equals in strife, equals in trying to keep a foothold in this fast spinning world, equals in the ability to laugh at adversity. Though this loss can never be laughed at.

My brother, the psychologist, is on his way to the office to counsel clients who either feel like pulling the plug, or who overeat, or even those who love too much.

'Pull over to the side of the road,' I tell him on the mobile. 'What is it! Tell me!'

'Have you pulled over?' I know he will think it's our father that something has happened to.

'All right, I've pulled over. Now what's happened?'

I then ring my teacher brother who must be in the office, for he comes immediately to the phone. 'I know,' he says, already crying when I begin the spiel of death. 'I know. I'm on my way.'

I continue the ring-around, but after those first two calls I don't remember who I speak to. It's like I'm reading a cue card: This is the nine o'clock news. Today a young man took his life. He was found by police in the backyard of the house where he lived with his grandmother. There are no suspicious circumstances. The young man had been diagnosed with schizophrenia, but it is believed in recent years he had been healthy and coping well with life. Some say a broken romance was the catalyst for his death. For funeral details, check local papers.

I delay calling the funeral parlour. If I can keep it all in the abstract, words not deeds, it just might turn out to be a mistake. Stupid really, for there's no mistaken identity, no CPR that'll bring you back. A funeral director is the one who brings the whole thing to a conclusion. He is the one who puts the nail in the coffin. The one who pushes the button and you'll slide out of sight, blue velvet drapes stopping us from seeing too much.

I hear the shower. Open the bathroom door a fraction. Steam fills the room. 'Are you okay?' I ask my youngest, whose tall, skinny body I can just make out behind the fogged screen. I can't make out what he says, but his tone sounds as though he wants me to go away. I leave the fan off. I, too, would prefer not to see clearly.

My other son is still in bed. 'What do we do now?' he asks when I go to check on him.

'Just help each other through this.'

'Will I get up? What do I do?'

'Have a shower and then come down to the kitchen. I'll be there.'

The Yellow Pages are open on the table. My husband has circled two local burial companies. I read them. Read them again. Is the advertisement with the bigger font a more caring organisation? Or should I go with the one that has a cross in the right-hand corner. I dither, not wanting an over-the-top 'you're-with-the-angels' service. Still, I choose the religious one when I remember what your Nan told me just that morning. Out of the blue, a couple of days ago, you'd been reading the paper and suddenly you turned to her, saying, with the most content of smiles, 'Nan, I now know Jesus does exist.' At the time she'd not thought it much of a statement. Of course, in hindsight...

He has such a soft voice the man who works for the company with a logo of a cross. He treats me as if I've a terminal disease. But then, death is terminal. He can come to the house early this afternoon. And would that be convenient, and would I be wanting a cremation or a burial? I need to think about that. You liked playing with fire, burnt the back fence down once. Then you torched a derelict wooden shack (or so you told your brother.) That's why you loved this house. It has a fireplace and you'd stack it full and sit on the hearth, face red from the heat. Poking, poking at the smoking wood. Playing with fire is different from being burnt to a cinder. Would it terrify you to sense the thud, thud of clay as it sealed you in forever? Some Islanders have the best way of sending off the dead. I'd like to do that. Put you in a canoe festooned with beer cans, and a Coke or two, and watch the current swirl you to nowhere. To everywhere.

I hear the shower start up again. My boys will be clean to face this day. I search for my husband. He's at the blind side of the house, sitting on the ground, beneath the clothesline.

'Come and sit with me.' His face has collapsed in onto itself.

I sit on the herringboned bricks and tell him he will get piles if he sits here too long. He tries to laugh, but it comes out like a moan.

11

'I feel so fucking useless,' he says. I wonder if he means right now, or is he thinking about the past.

Beneath lines of multi-coloured pegs, I hug my knees. Grey Cat sits on the wood box staring at the two people who look like they're hiding from the world. A lemon falls from the over-hanging tree and rolls, stopping at my feet. Strange it has fallen, for it is not yet ripe. 'The pull of gravity sometimes overrides reason,' I mutter, more to myself. I kick the lemon away. I hear tap, tap, tap on tin. The neighbour putting food out for the dog.

'Where are you going?' asks my husband, as if it's a normal part of our day to be sitting under the clothesline.

'To make breakfast. We have to eat.' I don't feel bad leaving him there beneath the clothesline that has no clothes. We all need time alone to let the truth settle.

Before I go inside, I light a cigarette and wander out the front. My favourite camellias are in bloom. Big ones. White with yellow centres like poached eggs. As I stand there blowing smoke to nowhere, I think of Grandfather. He had a huge, white camellia that shaded his bedroom window. It was the only beautiful thing he had in his last years.

My mouth tastes furry, like mould. I go inside, pour four glasses of orange juice. Never again shall I pour five. Youngest son comes to the table and stares at the newspaper. He turns it over to the sports section. Stares and stares. The doorbell. Women from my workplace. Each of them holds me tight as she cries, and I sense not just her sympathy, but her thankfulness it wasn't her child. I watch as my youngest drains the glass of juice and wish I had some special liquid to take away the drained look on his face.

And then it begins. Knocking and ringing; flowers delivered by poker-faced couriers whose expressions will change when they make their next deliveries that read Happy Birthday! Or Congratulations! A New Baby! instead of In Deepest Sympathy. Surprisingly, I find solace in the colours and perfume that fill so many corners of my house. Surprising because I feel emotionally shut down, yet those senses automatically kick in. Never again shall I send a donation to a foundation instead of flowers to the grieving.

Middle son takes a call from his tutor. I listen as he talks. The ease with which he tells her of his brother's death, his emotional distancing, worries me. Already I am keeping an extra close watch on him.

My brothers arrive, my father. All morning I'm hugged and patted and told they can't imagine what I'm feeling. Feeling? I'm not feeling anything! I see too much though; the death wink. I want to hold your last words; surely the coroner can take a photostat of the note for the death file.

Lunchtime, and FF, my Forever Friend arrives with food. Every action seems important to me; the way she shreds the lettuce, slices tomatoes, halves the rolls with one stroke of the knife. As she works, she takes the staysharp knives from where they are slotted in their wooden container and replaces them upside down. Seems these twenty years or so I have been putting them in the wrong way up, minimising their sharpness. Perhaps all along I've been doing things arse-up. I eat a tasteless roll, finishing it as the man in the conservative suit and the crooked hairpiece arrives to discuss details of your farewell. I try not to look at his hairpiece. Already I've forgotten his name.

We sit around the dining table like guests at a Tupperware party. Instead of celery storers, we look at body storers. We study the albums that hold photos of caskets. There's the deluxe, he tells us, and points out those with satin lining and copper handles, gold even, if we want. While he does his sales pitch I try to remember if you ever spoke of what to do. It's my youngest who speaks out.

'We can't burn him, Mum.'

'Right.' I don't question how he knows this, am just glad someone has made the decision for me. It's my youngest, too, who decides the quality of the casket.

13

'He wouldn't want us to spend a huge amount. He'd be cross if we did.'

'Yes. Yes,' I say.

So bogged down are we with death's weight, that we all eagerly acquiesce. I'm sure if one of us wanted gold llama as lining and go-kart wheels instead of pall-bearers, there'd be a chorus of, 'Yes, yes.'

When the party-plan concludes, the representative totes up the cost. While he discusses payment with my husband, through the dining room window I am surprised to see so many people in the yard, some sitting under the shade of the grapevine, others needing the sun's warmth. A neighbour offers mugs of drink and plates of food. A friend sits on the steps staring at the garden as if watching a rose bloom. My husband writes out a deposit cheque and I wonder at the need for such a down-payment. It's not as though we can change our minds. Oops, sorry, we've decided to defer the inevitable. The timing's just not right.

The man tugs at his wig, stands and gathers the albums. He sees himself out. For a time we sit at the table. The albums have left blurred squares in the dust. I must dust before the wake. Noise filters from outside; mobile phones ringing, subdued chatting, even an ambulance siren in the distance.

The four of us stand around the table as if waiting for a tour leader who's running late. 'I think we need a group hug,' I say. We anchor ourselves to each other. Someone's tears fall onto the carpet. 'The only way we'll get through this,' I say, 'is by screaming when we need to, crying wherever we are, and telling each other when we're scared.'

'Yes, yes,' they chorus.

Somehow the sun sets. I stand on the front porch, the sensor light turned off for I'm tired of being observed by people who search my face for signs I'm going under. Usually I find solace in the setting of the sun, the continuity it represents. Sort of another page turning. This time, as night swallows the saffron tinged sky,

I feel as though the last page has been turned. And though intellect tells me it's the end of a chapter not the book, my heart over-rides such rational thought.

I sit on the tiled steps and smoke cigarette after cigarette. Grey Cat rubs against my leg. The Greek neighbour comes running up the brick driveway, slippers flap, flap, flapping, pointing a spatula like a water diviner. 'Oh my God. Is it true? I've just heard!'

'Yes.'

'How did he…?'

'He hung himself.'

'Oh God, oh my God!'

She stands there, apron splattered by tomatoes, or blood. I wait for her to touch me, hold me against large breasts that will cushion my heavy head. Instead, she is the one who needs comforting, for she tells me of her son, and how worried she's been about him, and if he got a job everything would be all right. Then the flap, flap, flapping as she runs home to her son, and I'm left to ponder the correct grammar. Hung or hanged?

The sensor light comes on. 'Are you all right Mum?'

'Just getting a bit of fresh air.' I light another cigarette.

'When are you coming in?'

'Soon, Darling. Don't worry. I'm okay.'

Mozzies come in for the kill. I slap them away. I'll never be okay. The distance of time will make no difference. Dead is dead and no number of births will repair my shredded heart. Moths tango towards the light. There is no dance of death, just a shuffle, shuffle into the night that has no dawn.

Another courier working overtime presents me with flowers. I've run out of vases. A bucket will have to do. Too many flowers now. The house is starting to smell like a cemetery.

We go about doing the usual things like bringing the cats in for the night, deadlocking the front door. Even remember to clean our teeth. One time when habits are a lifesaver. I wash my face. Tonight my husband cleans his teeth too hard, and too long. The moisturiser I lather on my face is as cool as my mother's hand when I had a temperature.

'Sunless,' I say, staring into the mirror at my unfamiliar face.

'What?'

'That's what you become when you lose a son. Sunless.'

My husband stops brushing. Spits the paste and blood from his mouth. Goes to hold me. I push him away. It's like I need to suffer alone in order to pay you the highest respect.

We go to bed for there is nowhere else to go. Grey Cat nudges beneath the doona and settles in the curve of my legs. The crescent moon hangs crooked; sorrow throwing it off-kilter. The now stilled chaos of the day makes silence loud. A pressure cooker of a day. Droves of people milling through the house as if an 'Open for Inspection'. And we were on show; family scrutinising us for signs of breakage, friends darting glances of, 'if it can happen to them…' acquaintances trying to read between the lines, 'whose fault was it?'

Side by side we lie in bed, no talking – just breaths and sighs. I reach for my husband, using our special touch. 'Are you sure?' he asks. 'I have to,' I say. I need to feel something, anything. When he is inside me, I still can't feel.

An hour later, I'm still awake. Though I don't have a headache, I take two Mercindyls that normally knock me out for many hours. I sleep for a short while. Sit bolt upright. Listen, but can hear nothing. Grey Cat miaows at being disturbed. My husband snores mindlessly. What has woken me? The second my feet touch the carpet, my youngest calls, 'You okay, Mum?' Did I wake him or has he been on guard? I stand at his bedroom door, try to make out his shape. Am comforted by the fact that the sheet doesn't cover his head. 'Just going to make a chamomile tea. Do you want a sandwich? Glass of milk?'

'Nah. Don't be long though.'

Grey Cat, thinking it's time for breakfast, follows me to the kitchen and jumps into the pantry. Sits amongst the tins of cat food, narrow eyes adjusting to the fluorescent light. The kettle boils, switches itself off. I stare at the diamanté-scattered sky. Where are you now? When eventually I pour the water, it's lukewarm. I take the tea into the dining room and sit at the mahogany table. The green brochure the Coroner gave me lies beside the vase of dried hydrangeas. I read about autopsies. Will they be cutting you now? Straight down the middle? Side to side? Disembowelling? All the time wondering whose son you were and where you fitted in the scheme of things. Or, why you didn't fit in the scheme of things. Read that a death certificate will not be issued until the cause of death is known. I'd have thought a rope mark scored around the neck was pretty obvious.

I rock myself, hands cradling my stomach. The pain of childbirth measures nothing against the pain of your death.

Dust, so much dust on the table. My fingers leave a trail as if racing snails have suddenly disappeared. When I have read the brochure back to front, then front to back, I go to the kitchen and light a cigarette. I return to the dining room. Stop short at what has happened in my absence. Glitter. Gold glitter sprinkled from the middle of the table to where I'd been sitting. Snail trails full of glitter. Your spiritual caress. I cup the glitter; rub it over my face, drowning myself in the knowledge that where you are, it's a place of beauty.

Glitter! So unlike you. But then hanging was so unlike you, too.

Chapter 2

If a story is to have a beginning, mine began that summer of 1969 when I spent most of it going to the toilet checking for blood; that tell-tale sign of barrenness. There I'd sit willing that magical stain to appear like a rabbit out of a hat. Hours on that toilet staring fate in the face.

'Congratulations!' said the Indian doctor in his pappadam voice when the report came back. The rabbit had died. He started counting up the weeks while I just sat there wondering how I could take a day off work so no-one else would be as surprised as I was. I would have had an abortion if I'd had the know-how to do the illegal unthinkable. A girlfriend had paid ten pounds for a tablet that did nothing but make her puke. Another drank a bottle of gin whilst sitting in a hot bath but all that happened was a hot-hangover.

Over the next few months I went to work feeling nauseous – more from fear than morning sickness. As a secretary for a cosmetics company, I had many tools to camouflage the pastiness, to paint a picture of what I didn't feel.

When I was able to face my parents with the news, Dad's eyebrows collided from horror. As usual, Mum tried to save the day with, 'You can get married. The baby will be early. That's all there is to it.' She smiled the thin smile she saved for family traumas.

The thing was, I didn't want to marry the father, hadn't even thought about a baby. If I had, I'd want to conceive on white satin sheets instead of the dusty, vinyl seat of a ute. When the child was born I'd be eighteen. I'd been saving for three years to go overseas. Now I couldn't even save myself.

As usual I did the right thing by everyone. Just a registry office wedding, followed by a counter-lunch at the local pub, alcohol numbing the fact we were all nearly strangers. Hemmed in between my new in-laws and husband, I watched as they attacked their T-bones and guzzled beer. How did I get to this? Simply a quickie to stave off boredom then, hey presto, a lengthy life of crass boredom!

I studied this man who was a double for Burt Reynolds, yet who had the personality of Boris Karloff, and wondered how I'd be able to live with a movie star who bored me witless. He was a preening cock, seemingly delighted with the way things had turned out.

I made the best of things; I was the proverbial little missus up the duff. I wasn't much of a cook, though I tried to impress. The first time the in-laws came to dinner I studied each mouthful they took, counted the number of times they chewed, imagined the veal sliding down their throats causing internal bleeding. The reason for my concern was that I'd flattened the schnitzels by using a milk bottle. Banged away till it smashed to smithereens. Hunched over, so my husband wouldn't notice, I'd tweezered every glass sliver from the veal. At least, I hoped I had. The in-laws left when the beer ran out. For hours after, I lay awake imagining a post-mortem that would reveal they'd died of internal haemorrhaging, imagining my baby would be a prison baby.

In my parents' house, the cracked walls of my bedroom were covered with posters of The Beatles, and African violets grew in pots on the windowsill. Mum let me paint the walls of my room indigo and canary yellow. The rented flat I now lived in looked like an operating theatre. Sterile and spartan. Just a couch and a coffee table in the lounge. Its mouldy walls I'd painted acrylic white.

My husband easily settled into married life, but then I would too if all I had to do was move my belongings to another place and yet still find a meal on the table at the appropriate time, dunnies cleaned, beer in the fridge. Changing Mum for a wife was as easy for him as changing shoes. Whereas I'd been sold into slavery, two for the price of one.

Night after night, weeks going into months, I'd sit at the table watching my husband shovel food into his mouth, listening to his day's activities. He never asked about my day. I could understand I didn't have much to say after I left work, but I could've brightly coloured the day in for him if he'd bothered to ask.

My husband worked in Real Estate. Not as a salesman as he'd first led me to believe. What he did, I found out after we were married, was hammer in 'For Sale' signs.

Each evening would start out with me asking, 'How was your day?'

While he stepped out his day for me, I'd mentally continue his conversation, finishing the same old sentences before he spoke them…' There's nothing worse than trying to bang on clay. That takes forever. And as I'm paid on commission, blah blah blah'. Scintillating stuff. Then he'd turn the telly on and be mesmerised by the game shows. Until my stomach grew so big and I couldn't comfortably fit behind my desk, I hadn't gone on each night about how many words a minute I could type, how many errors I'd made and how long it took to complete a Profit & Loss statement.

Anyway, a silent lesson I'd learnt from Mum was to keep my needs to myself. Men weren't all that interested in knowing how you ticked over. All they were interested in was you always being available to them, and supplying the food, not necessarily in that order. Unconsciously I copied Mum's behaviour. Always three vegetables and meat every night, and giving him the best piece of meat. Going without so I could pay the bills. How easily I fell into this trap of denying myself. But then not so unusual when you grow up with a mother who once in a blue moon would buy herself a cheap cotton dress from Coles. I'd watch rapt as she'd loosen her long hair from the pink plastic curlers, put the floral dress on, then paint her lips ruby red. 'This, old thing?' she'd say when my father, suitably impressed, asked if it was a new dress. 'Had it for years!' Watching her play out this charade over many years, I began to wonder if she denied her new dresses because she felt she didn't deserve to look pretty. I didn't have to enact such scenes as my husband never said I looked pretty. In fact, as my body began to look more and more like a watermelon with limbs, he'd say, 'I wish you would always be fat. Then no other man would ever look at you.'

There was so much I needed to talk about and no-one to talk with. Nothing world shattering, just the fact that I felt so alienated from the person I used to be. The one who went dancing in the halter neck that shimmered and shook as she did. Not the one who sat in a sterile flat incubating a dancing baby. It was no use having a deep and meaningful with Mum about my situation for it had been decades since she'd stopped dancing to have six babies. And the only real friend who was my age, was pretty much in the same boat. And without any oars.

One hot summer's night, about a month before my baby was born, I lay awake for hours trying hard to ignore the way my husband's nose quivered and his throat vibrated from the guttural snores. I hugged the pillow to me, afraid I'd swaddle his face with it.

Alarmed at the strength of my feelings, I left the bed. In the bathroom I didn't know what to do. I didn't need to pee, no pimples to pop. I pulled myself onto the twin-spin washing machine. Buddha-like I sat there. Felt my baby for reassurance. Found what felt like an arm. Tried to hold its hand, but the dancer had retired for the night. Everyone asleep but me. Hiccupping sobs came from nowhere. What was the matter with me? So what if I didn't have anyone to enjoy a sunset with. For the first time since the Indian doctor had congratulated me, I yearned for the birth of my child. Perhaps I could wonder at life again when it was born.

'I know how to make that baby come,' Mum said the fifth morning of a February heat wave and I was three weeks' overdue. 'We'll walk him out.' And so for hours up and down High Street we strolled, window-shopping at the haberdashery, buying coffee scrolls from the bakery, reading the faded menus stuck in the window of the Chinese takeaways that seemed so cosmopolitan to us then. In the sweltering heat I mistook the rivulets of water that ran down my legs for perspiration.

That night my husband told me to go back to sleep when I tried to wake him.

'Come on! Now! They're two minutes apart.'

Still he refused to wake. I timed it so I got the suitcase out to the car between contractions. The empty whisky bottle on the table made me think it'd be safer to drive myself. I jangled the keys at his ear. This time he roused himself enough to realise I wasn't doubled over from laughing.

Much too slowly he drove up Sydney Road. 'Hurry! Hurry! Please hurry.' Along the way he pointed out the opposition's For Sale signs, when all I wanted to do was hang one around his neck.

'I'll go to Mum's and wait,' he said, once he'd carried my bag into Emergency. He thought I was waving him off, but it was like I was swatting away at a fly.

The cranky sister insisted she stick an enema up me, that 'first babies don't come so quick'. Within the hour I was bearing down. Shit streamed out of me onto the bloodied sheets. Then my baby poured himself out. Over the bulge of my stomach, all I saw was how blue you were. The doctor untangled the cord from around your neck. You were whisked away beyond the swinging doors. 'To be monitored,' the sister told me as she tried not to breathe in the shit smell.

Hours later, the sound of babies crying. A trolley with babies aligned like packs of jubes was pushed into the ward where new mothers eagerly waited. I peered, tried to pick out my baby. Six mothers. Only five babies. The other mothers unbuttoned nighties, latching hungry babies onto breasts that leaked just from the sound of their wails. The fifth mother crossed her arms, refused her baby. Said she was going back to work and wanted her baby bottle fed.

'They're not there for show, you know!' said the nun, forcing that baby into its mother's arms.

'Here's your baby.' A nurse who looked like she was just out of school handed me a tin cup and hand pump. Not for me the sucking of lips on yearning nipples, but the squish, squelch of rubber that drained me of nurture; the clanking of tin against the glass phial that held me to ransom against fulfilment.

At the next feeding time, and the next and the next, with other mothers oohing and aahing over their perfect images, I hand-pumped my milk. In and out, in and out. My wrist hurt. But more than that, I felt as though a vacuum was sucking out my innards that kept me upright. As I disintegrated, I sobbed. Mothers clung to their babies; one even covered her child's face with a blanket. A nun came running, steered by the black habit that sailed behind her. She took me in a wheelchair to the Intensive Care Nursery. Through the glass cage I watched your heaving chest. My hand just fitted through the glass circle. I was afraid if I touched you for too long the oxygen would escape and your little chest would shudder even more from the effort of staying alive.

After I was discharged, for weeks I bounced along in the 203 bus, all the while thinking the expressed milk would curdle and be of no use to you. Twice a day I got off at the hospital where Jesus hung on a wooden cross and which bore no resemblance to my suffering. And twice a day I returned to the sterile flat with its empty cot.

And then the day came.

'Go on, lift him out. He won't break,' the sister said, holding open the lid.

Gingerly I picked you up, cradled you to my heavy breasts. Waited for the surge of bonding I'd heard other mothers talk about. Suddenly it was me who couldn't get a breath. Such a feeling. A virgin being deflowered by love's force. And though I was a non-believer, I somehow understood how Mary was a virgin until she had Jesus.

You were unsettled from the start. Though when you gave me that crooked smile it made up for the hours of lost sleep that made me drowsy from fatigue.

It was me that did everything for you. If my husband wasn't banging in For Sale signs he was watching the footy, going to the pub, or drinking himself stupid at home. It got so, I was functioning on just a couple of hours' sleep. Mum told me to put treacle on your dummy if you woke during the night and that way I'd get a decent sleep.

The day I stopped the treacle bribe was when I woke one morning to see you staring back at me, just one eye open. During the night, I'd put the dummy into what I thought was your mouth. I cried and laughed and hugged you to me and took away the blink by licking the treacle from the eyelid that trembled from the touch of my tongue. If ever there was a moment when I truly bonded with you, it was then. Thirty years later when I held your lifeless body you again had one eye closed. Winking at me as if life had been one big joke.

There was such naked joy in watching you grow, how the sun fell on your new skin that was still peeling from being too long in my womb, tiny veins that coursed with my blood, nails that grew quicker than any other part of you. And the rituals…biting down your nails because my teeth were safer than scissors…spitting on the cowlick that refused to lay flat…daily swabbing the stump of cord with methylated spirits. The day the black stump detached itself I cried for we were no longer physically bound together. Yet I was happy that you were free to be yourself. There were other rituals too, like preparing formulas to supplement my milk, the daily grind of washing nappies, cleaning every orifice with cotton balls and cotton buds and bum wipes. Washing your little penis, marvelling at how you'd get an erection whenever I pulled the foreskin back for a thorough clean.

One night, six weeks after the birth, my husband returned from his usual watering hole. When he climbed into bed his heavy body weighted the mattress to his side of the bed. I hung onto the edge so I wouldn't roll into him. My parents had the right idea. Their bed was old, sagging in the middle. Dad put a wooden door across the frame so's they wouldn't roll into each other.

'Have you made the appointment?' he asked, yet again. A nudge in the back, then, 'Have you?!'

I rolled over, pretended sleep. He pulled the blanket off me. 'I asked you a question!'

'I can't bring myself to do it.'

'No son of mine is going to be different.'

'Boring world if we were all the same.'

'If you don't do it, I will.'

'There's a new school of thought…'

'There's nothing to think about!'

I pulled the blanket over my head. He pulled me to him. I knew not to resist. He was only trying to make a point, as brief as it was. When he'd finished filling me up like a bottle of clag, I rolled to the far side of the bed. His foot kicked the back of my knee. Reflexively my leg kicked out into nothing, his kick a reminder of what I had to do.

The next week, delaying the inevitable, I slowly walked to the surgery. You stared at the movement outside the pram. You really smiled now, a 'hey, I trust you,' kind of smile. As I turned into the doctor's surgery, the wind skipped fallen leaves and there was a rumble in the distance.

There was no-one in the waiting room for mine was the last appointment of the day.

'You go shopping for a while,' said the doctor.

'It's okay, I'll wait here.'

'Best you go shopping and come back in an hour.'

I did as the demi-god told me.

I waited at the top of the lane. Rain pelted down but I didn't run for cover, couldn't move, just watched the large hand on my watch. After forty minutes I could wait no longer. The receptionist was locking the files and the doctor had changed into shorts and long socks. You were lying on your back in the pram. Your sobs bit into me. 'Try not to get it wet. If it gets infected bring him back straightaway; otherwise, Panadol should do the trick,' said the doctor.

I pushed you up the hill to Mum's. You sobbed even harder at the jarring of the pram as I dragged it up the six steps to the front door.

'It's the best thing, Luv,' said Mum, as I held your trembling body close to me. 'Your brothers have all had it done.'

'That doesn't make it right!'

'Well, look at your uncle. He never had it done and a few years back it all swelled up, as painful as hell. Turned out he didn't know he had to pull the foreskin back and so it got infected.'

'Jesus, he's over eighty! If he went that long without cleaning it, that just goes to show!'

'You wouldn't want your son being the laughing-stock in the boys' change-room. Now how about a cuppa?'

For hours you sobbed, unable to catch your breath, to drink, or be soothed with cuddles. Such irony. You'd only recently shed your physical link to me, the stump of the umbilical cord, only to be initiated into the world of men.

Chapter 3

Over the next few days, the sun continues to rise, the kettle boils on demand, and my sons take too long under the shower. I'm left with no hot water to warm the shiver that's settled in my body. Everyone must be able to see how I constantly shudder. A stuttering body, tripping over itself.

The next stranger to come into our house is the celebrant. She goes on about how the ceremony will be a celebration of your life. On the surface I go along with her way of thinking, but inside I wrestle with this description. I never have before, but always mutely accepted the invitation extended at the end of every funeral service…' John and Betty would like you all to come along to their home to celebrate their mother's life.' The death of an old person is a celebration, for they have had time to fulfil most of their desires. You, my son, were just getting a taste of desire. It's difficult to celebrate when weighted from unshed tears.

I almost sink from these tears that can't be measured like a barrel of beer or a case of spuds can. In my youth I was once heartbroken over a romance. My heart then was so heavy I expected it to fall out, and plop onto the floor. Everyone would see my despair. The difference now is that this weight pervades every sinew making it forever impossible to grasp, dislodge.

On Thursday I wake, knowing this day is to be the last occasion I share with you. It should be raining. In the movies it rains at funerals; mourners with umbrellas and dark coats matching the cloud of fear it could be them next time.

Silently we eat breakfast. There is just the crunch of Sustain.

The four glasses of orange juice remain untouched for our stomachs are soured enough.

When we are dressed in our best suits, I gather my family together, tell them we must go into the yard and cut a branch off the apricot tree. The sombreness of the day doesn't allow for superfluous words, and so they don't ask why. They don't know the significance of the apricot tree. They only know it was your tree.

Beneath a birdless sky we each have a turn at sawing the branch. This year the tree will prolifically fruit for the first time. Last year it bore just a couple of apricots that fell to the ground before they had a chance to ripen. We became like anxious parents, you and I, waiting five years for your tree to give us a return on our investment. This summer the fruit will ripen as you rot in the ground. My sons carry the branch into the kitchen and lay it on the table. I stay with your tree. Pick many of the almond-sized apricots, gently place them into the raffia bag I've emptied of junk. When the limousine pulls up to deliver us to the place where you wait for us, I'm still leaning against the trunk your hand easily spanned.

The chauffeur drives much too slowly to the funeral parlour. Such a stupid name, parlour, as if we're about to take tea in the front room with friends. We stare out the window, seeing the same things differently now. I cradle the apricot branch as I once held you.

We're an hour early for we want to spend time with you. In a room off the chapel, you lie in the mahogany box dressed in your best. The blue shirt is buttoned to the collar. Makeup camouflages the rawness, though I can still see the line circling your throat. Such a fucking simple line that sucked your soul to somewhere we can't share. You're not winking now.

I lean over, kiss your eyes, nose, mouth. Suddenly happiness seizes me. 'Look, they've made a mistake! He's crying. He's not dead.' But it's my tears that fall onto your eyes and trickle down your olive skin. My heart will never beat in rhythm again.

Like the Egyptians, we've bought gifts to send you on your way.

I place between your cold fingers one of my favourite earrings. The amethyst that swings against my cheek when I laugh. I keep its mate, for in this way, no matter the distance between us, I will always be able to hold a part of what you hold.

From your father, though he didn't offer anything, on the satin lining I place the pack of ABC playing cards left over from his childhood. I have nothing else of his to give you. I was keeping them so your child would have something tangible from that family tree.

My second son offers a gift of your tired old cricket hat. He slips the Walkman in the crook of your arm.

My youngest places a packet of Drum tobacco, and a box of matches, in your suit pocket.

My husband lays a stubby of beer alongside you. 'In case you get thirsty,' he whispers.

My letter to you, written just last night, I leave beneath your crossed hands, close to your heart.

The hour is filled with us whispering to you. Whispers of regrets, and promises. Your shirt is splattered with our tears.

'It's time,' says the man with a voice modulated and well-rehearsed for a group such as us. 'We must close the lid.'

'Let them wait. Just a few more minutes.' Just a few more lifetimes, I say to myself.

I cannot delay any more. The chapel is full of watchful mourners who, without a coffin to focus on, must wonder if they have come to the right place.

Then you are gone. So quietly they screw the lid into place. I'd imagined hammers.

'No,' begs my youngest. 'Please, open it!'

This is what I've dreaded. One of us refusing to say goodbye.

'You must open it. I forgot this!' He waves a packet of tobacco papers.

The suited man, nonplussed, looks to me. I give a determined nod.

No gift could ever be as precious as the opportunity each of us had to kiss you once more.

The door opens. There is hushed silence. As we escort you into the chapel, muffled sobs escape from mourners as they see how my youngest suffers so. I want to reach out across the coffin to touch him, but my arms are too heavy.

The celebrant stands at the rostrum, her face a blank arrangement. The man in the suit places my favourite flowers, Christmas lilies, on top of the coffin. I put the bough of the apricot alongside the lilies. The one and only cricket trophy you finally scored at the age of twenty-eight, I display on the floor, in front of the coffin.

There could be twelve mourners or thousands. The actress doesn't see anyone. Not even when she stands at the rostrum to give the eulogy. She reads her lines from a copy of the letter she placed on her son's chest. It is so very important to her she doesn't break down, doesn't let the weight of unshed tears detract from the importance of his being.

Some of the words from the script rebound, leaving an echo, but the actress refuses to let words like loyalty, compassion, forgiveness, cause her to stumble or stop, even when she speaks of that last holiday they spent together. She and her son sitting on the banks of the Murray, a line in one hand, a stubby in the other. Of how, as the year turned over beneath a full moon, they shared a bottle of champers. Not once does she falter. Not once, until she says what isn't scripted, 'From the time he became ill, he shadowed me. Every time I turned around, he was there. I'll miss his shadow.'

She sits down in her navy blue suit bought on sale last year. Perfect for funerals, she told her friend who'd questioned why she needed a power suit when she'd left the corporate world. She is never going to tempt fate with throwaway lines like that again, never going to read the obituaries last thing at night after she's done the crossword. For the last six months, she's searched out what read like suicides. Was that psychic right all those years ago, calling her a medium, saying she should hone the skill? She should have listened to the psychic.

As the song fades to nothing, middle son takes his place at the rostrum. I listen attentively as he talks of brotherly things like the first girlie magazine you gave him, saying, 'Don't let your little brother see this. He's not ready for it, yet.' Your face keeps getting in the way, and I miss what else my son has to say about his big brother. Though I hear the last sentence. 'I don't approve of what you did, but I must respect you for it.' Only twenty years old and already middle son is learning the cruellest of lessons.

Others come forward to say a few words, and a few words is all some men with broad shoulders can say, for the remainder of their words get gulped down as tears fall onto their face, their ties. My psychologist brother tries to speak, but all he can manage is...' We walked in the Blackwood Forest...we walked in the forest...' My teacher brother blubbers as he talks about me, my strength. As he leaves the rostrum he gives me a framed music sheet of Lennon and McCartney's song, *Let it Be*. Your cricket coach tells of the time he met you. How after training he was locking up the club rooms and found you outside, asleep on the steps. At the age of twenty-seven, you'd finally stockpiled enough belief in yourself to return to your first love. But you shouldn't have called into the pub on the way.

I remember that day, the Grand Final. Your stepfather and I sat on collapsible chairs at the edge of the oval. Positioned ourselves to be in line with you as you ran to the crease. The power of your spin-bowling! With each wicket you took, you'd turn and look to me. You could've been that little kid who fronted up all those years on a Saturday morning ready to do damage to the opposition, and always looking to mum for recognition. 'Best on the Field' is inscribed on the trophy beneath the casket.

'Best Anywhere' is my inscription for you. 'It's bigger than any my brothers have got,' you told your uncle. How very glad your brothers are your trophy is bigger than any they've received.

The coach takes the trophy, kisses it, and puts it on the coffin. 'Such a great bloke,' he says, more to himself.

Your father utters not a word. I rang him just a few nights ago, and asked if there was anything he wanted included in the eulogy I was writing. 'Nah, just tell him I love him.' 'And you'll be a pall-bearer?' I asked. 'Nah couldn't think of nothin' worse. I was one at me mate's years back and I had nightmares for ages. Nah, couldn't stomach that.'

As the men in my family gather around you, your father sits there. Ears full of silver studs that he'd spent more time getting pierced than he ever had for his son.

Middle son beckons to your father to get up, to do this last thing for you. Still he resists. Middle son insists. I wish he didn't for I feel your father hasn't earnt the right to carry you.

My hand resting on the coffin, slowly I make my way up the aisle. So many people. Standing room only. All here because they love you. Why didn't they swamp you with love while you were alive?

I pass your favourite uncle, your drinking mate. He looks at the floor, hanky clutched in his hand. You spent your last weekend with him, sitting up all night drinking, and the more you skulled whisky, the more you talked of killing yourself. When you surfaced the next day with not even a hangover, as was normal for you, your uncle confronted you with what you'd said. You couldn't remember. Wouldn't even think such a thing. Your uncle and his wife decided it had been grog talking. If only they'd told me before you acted out those drunken thoughts.

The aisle seems to have no end. Someone grabs my wrist. My dearest aunt. She pulls me to her. Though I want to suffocate in her ample breasts, I pull away, angry she has distracted me from walking beside you.

Outside I sit in the limousine behind the one where you lie adorned with flowers. If anyone touches me, speaks to me, I will scream forever. They stand, the mourners, crowding the doorway, spilling outside, peering at the tinted windows that shield me. I don't want their sympathy, their attention. Nothing must distract me from this, your last journey.

Two for the price of one. That's what the Tupperware dealer said we might as well do; no extra cost to dig deeper. Hundreds of gum trees surround this sacred place. Wind rustles the leaves. A bird caw caws overhead. Within me there is a frozen silence no wind will ever pierce.

My sons lead the procession to where I am standing on the hill. My youngest, face twisted from grief, still cries. My middle son is stoic, as stoic as the day you left home those fifteen years ago. Again and again I asked, 'Are you sure this is what you want?' Then the doorbell. I hand the suitcase to your father before he can put a foot inside and soil my home. As his car putt-putted up the hill, you stared out the back window like one of those dogs with a nodding head. Except, your head was still, eyes looking at me, through me. I still waved when you would have been a mile out of sight. Must stay in remote control. Wash the floor. Water the plants. Hang the washing out. As I peg nappies on the line, not stretching too high for my last child is nearly ready to be born, middle son wakes from an afternoon sleep. There he stands, a shadow behind the screen door, Snoopy under one arm, nappy at half-mast. 'Where's my bruvver? I want my bruvver.' I'd said nothing to him about you leaving us.

Slowly, so slowly, they lower you into the ground. The man in the navy suit butchers a wreath as he offers a flower to the mourners who, one by one, toss them onto your coffin, as if an afterthought. The last thing, the very last thing I have to offer you are the green apricots. I drop handfuls onto mahogany that shines like Great-Aunt's piano lid.

It should be raining. You liked the rain. No raincoat or prissy umbrella for you. Instead, baring yourself to the symphony of the storm that must, sometimes, have mirrored the zigzagging tremors in your mind. An echo that made you not so alone. Yes, it should be raining. Instead the sun shines dissolving the mourners' fear of death as if a figment of their imagination. You were not a figment of my imagination but a filigree. Fragile, transparent, yet…so whole.

And then the finale that has no encore. Wake, such a stupid name. More like a wake-up call. A, *This Could Be Your Life*. Sandwiches and finger food. And sausage rolls I'd frozen for a special occasion. As fingers reach for those perfect sausage rolls, it's as if they're taking a piece of you from me. You would make them by the dozens when you were at a loose end. You leant over the bench too low for your height. Concentrated so hard on piping the filling onto the pastry, then cutting each one exactly to size. The filling, not just sausage meat, but grated carrot, onion, zucchini, cheese. They'd melt in my mouth, just as you melted my heart. As I offer them around I tell no-one this is the last batch you made. When only a few remain on the oval plate, I hide them at the back of the fridge.

I'm on the balcony, watching the crowd mill below when Dad comes and stands beside me.

'Been looking for you,' he says.

'Just having a quiet moment.'

He cries. Wipes his face with his shirt sleeve. 'I've cried enough today. No more tears.' He puts an arm around my shoulders. 'You'll be okay. You'll get over this. Hell, I've lost mates in the war. You get over it.'

'You've got no idea! He was my son. He grew inside me. His heartbeat mirrored mine. He fed off me. Anything I felt he did too. Millions and millions of seconds of his life I was the one that sustained him. He wasn't a fucking mate. He was my son!'

'I'm sorry…I didn't mean…'

'And it didn't end with his belly button drying up. These last ten years it's been like he was in my womb again, sucking on my strength. As if we'd been rejoined.'

'Shhh…'

'Don't fucking shush me!' People stare up from the garden, but I don't care. 'And do you think I wanted that? Wanted my adult son to need me so much? But see, he had no choice. There was no-one else he trusted that way. His fucking father was useless.'

'I guess he did his best.'

I take the stubby from my father, suck on it, then toss it over the balcony where it lands in a bush. I wanted it to land on the concrete and smash to smithereens, to sound like I was feeling.

'All his father cared about were his de factos and their children.' I light another cigarette. 'My son rang me about three years ago. "Mum," he said, "I was just sitting here thinking. Dad's never taken me on a holiday, not ever. I was just thinking about that this afternoon. Not even a weekend away. He takes his de factos' kids, Mum, but never me." '

'Surely, not…'

'Oh, yes! Surely yes. You remember when he left me to go and live with his father? You know where he slept? Down the backyard in a caravan. Not in the warm house with its three bedrooms, but relegated down near the back fence because the bedrooms were being used by his father's imitation family; his de facto and her kids. And her kids had to have a bedroom each.'

'Well, did you say something?'

'I didn't say it loud enough.'

'That's not like you.'

Oh yes, it is Dad. If you only knew the fear, and revulsion, I had for his father. But I don't tell Dad what I'm thinking.

When the crowd disperses to face life again, and my family has gone to bed to escape life, I'm left with sandwiches with curled up corners. After I've made the house spotless, I clean out the fridge, do a load of washing, then a basket of ironing, and put the rubbish out. Anything to stop myself looking at the huge notice board filled with the many faces of you. A photo collage your brothers put together.

I try the telly. There's a movie about Wyatt Earp and just seconds into watching Mel Gibson, he is strung up to a tree, ready for hanging. I throw the remote control at the television; it misses and hits the brick hearth. Pieces scatter; the television turns off.

With nothing else to do, I sit on the patio beneath the bare grape-vine that sometimes shelters me. Slowly, slowly, I eat what's left of your sausage rolls. There's blood on my fingers and I'm surprised I haven't felt the pain of the bitten-down quicks. I sit there staring into the spotless house where the clock on the oven flashes HELP.

Chapter 4

The night it happened everything started out normally. It's only right that when a life-road comes to a dead-end, something grand should be scored in history to mark that last journey.

Coming home from work, I'd battled the traffic, giving the finger to a guy who was turning left from a right-hand lane. When he returned the digit, I did a Mrs Bobbitt, scissoring fingers at him, before accelerating away from road-rage.

Nothing unusual, either in juggling the washing and cooking a meal, while the cats did S-bends around my legs.

Corned beef with mustard sauce, boiled potatoes, beans and broccoli. I see the meal as clearly as I see the hand in front of me. I followed that up with left-overs from work. Lemon Delicious. It was like a 'Housewife's Reprieve' when the residents weren't in an eating mood and the chef bagged what hadn't been served.

I don't recall specifics of what the four of us said as we ate. Probably comfortable questions of, 'How was your day?' or 'Did you pick up the dry-cleaning?' or 'Did you hand the assignment in?' The corned beef was too salty, but the pudding was perfectly tart.

As I stacked the dishwasher and wiped the table, I nodded and nodded as my husband went on about the lack of accountability he was confronted with each day at work. His job is trailing figures on paper. It suits his personality, pedantic, needing everything to align and balance.

I checked the clock on the far wall. Just under an hour till *The Sopranos* started – a show I was well and truly hooked on.

Probably because it portrayed the Mafia bosses as boringly normal once they closed their door on the world. Playing at family life, just like the rest of us. If I got cracking, I could whip through the ironing in time to watch the show.

I was folding up the ironing board when the phone went. *The Sopranos* theme had just started. Please, nobody want me. Middle son's footsteps as he thumped down the hallway. 'Well, Big Bro, see you soon, then. Here's Mum.'

There went the viewing highlight of my week. Always when you phoned, our conversations were long. I sighed, felt short-changed. Why were you phoning now? I was to pick you up in the morning. We'd have all day to catch up. I took the phone outside so I could have a cigarette while we chatted.

'Hi, Darling. How're things?'

'Yeah, okay. Okay.'

'What're you doing?'

'Trying to get through a bottle of brandy.'

You didn't sound as though you'd been drinking. Usually I could tell if you had. Either my antennae were bent, or you were exaggerating.

'I was hanging out with a mate this arvo. Smoked a couple. Shared a bottle of whisky. Had some tea.'

It was good you'd gone out, for you'd spent too much time hanging around waiting in case your ex-girlfriend rang and wanted to get back together. So many times over the last few weeks you'd knocked back an invitation to come over and stay with us awhile, at least have dinner with us. Each time you'd insisted on staying close to the phone.

'What did you have?'

'Some dope.'

'For tea, I mean.'

'Oh, pizza. Listen, Mum. I found out today she's got another man. Had one for months. Kept us both going, and then dropped me. Why wasn't she honest, Mum? I wrote her all these letters.

I thought it was my fault, that something was wrong with me. I would've done anything for her.'

'Oh, Darling, there's nothing wrong with you…'

'All those letters and waiting around. Shit, Mum, it cuts so deep.'

I had only my love to offer as solace, second-rate compared to what you'd had with her. I told you there were more fish in the sea, and that life does go on, and, hey, look at your uncle. He thought he'd never get over it. We've all lost what we thought was our greatest love.'

'But you don't understand!'

'Listen to your mum, there's another woman out there just for you. I promise you that.'

'She was my soul-mate. I loved her. I'll never love anyone else.'

'Course you will. There's not one amongst us who hasn't had their heart broken at some time or another. You get over it. You think you won't ever be able to breathe again without it hurting, but you do, trust me.'

What else did I say, did you say, about love gone wrong? I only remember words that either take an edge off my guilt or beat me up.

'I saw the doctor this week,' you said. 'Gave me some sleeping tablets.'

'Did they help?'

'For a short while.'

It cuts so deep, began to play over and over in my mind. 'Listen, I'm coming across now. Sounds like you need to spend a week with us.'

'Nah, don't.'

'We can still have our day out tomorrow.'

'Nah, really, I'm going to sleep. I'm tired.'

'Are you going to take a sleeping tablet?'

'Course not. I've been drinking. You don't mix grog with drugs.'

And that was the line that made me think you were okay. Rational.

'Are you sure I can't come over right now?'

'Yeah, I'm fine. She's just broken my heart.'

'Listen, Darling, I'll be over first thing in the morning.'

'I might be asleep then.'

'So…I'll wake you, you duffer!'

One of us said, I love you. I think it was me. I usually finished our conversations with that. I don't remember you saying you loved me, but I think you did. I want to have that, at least. As I hung up the phone, I looked at the clock. Good. I'd catch the last half hour of The Sopranos.

'What's up?' said my husband as I sat down beside him.

'He's feeling down. Just found out she was two-timing him. I wanted to go pick him up now, instead of the morning, but he doesn't want me to.'

'Should you?'

For a moment, just a moment, I thought on whether I should. A part of me wanted to grab the car keys and rush to you. I reminded myself you were nearly thirty and didn't need a mollycoddling mother. This time there were no voices in your head warping your sense of reality. Just life nipping at your heels.

'No,' I said, 'he insists I don't. I've got to respect that.'

Though I watched a christening and a killing on the last half of The Sopranos, I was thinking of you. Always before, when your illness had taken hold, I instinctively knew when you needed me. I would go to you and we'd sit it out together, or I'd bring you home for a few weeks, even have you hospitalised if the terrors became too invasive. This time, though, you were healthy, had been for a couple of years. Anyway, if you'd been drinking as much as you said, if I travelled over now, by the time I got there I'd never be able to wake you. You'd be a dead-weight.

When the show finished, I took the cats outside beneath the crescent moon hanging like a dangly earring. I was already planning tomorrow. How I'd probably have to wake you, even if I got there at ten o'clock. Shopping first. Buy you some trackie daks – comfort was always your priority. A counter-lunch. An hour playing the pokies. Then home with us for the weekend, at least.

In bed I balanced the thick library book on my chest while I lost myself in someone else's sad life, and then I slept.

When I replay our last conversation, as I do over and over, I wonder if I've got the inflections right, and that I interpreted your answers correctly. Did I miss a clue that would've alerted me? There is one sentence I can't fit into the conversation, but which I know you uttered, as if a throw-away line. I phoned Lifeline last week. Words I haven't told anyone. Too ashamed that I didn't zero in on your desperation. I think I said something like, 'did they help?' You said, 'Yeah, they were good'. Why did not alarm bells ring? I'd always been your lifeline; the person you turned to when you fell off your bike, or when the devil tangoed in your head. The mere fact that you'd been searching for another lifeline should have alerted me, and there was another sentence you let slip. 'Nan wants me to move out in a couple of weeks'. 'So you'll come here,' I said, knowing you wouldn't want to. 'It doesn't matter, it's not important', was how you shrugged the dilemma away. Was it not important because you'd already decided you weren't going to be alive to worry about where you'd live? Nana's threat didn't unduly concern me, as at least twice a year she got her wind up about you drinking too much grog. And your flippant, 'it doesn't matter, it's not important', was typical of that possible scenario because we both knew her edict was just her way of letting off steam. Even knowing that, I still berate myself for not biting on those one-liners you lured me with. Fly fishing in an empty pool is such a solitary existence.

You loved fishing. In a photo I took of you just months before you died, you are in gumboots, standing on the beach at Wye

River, staring out to sea, patiently waiting for that elusive yank on the line. While you fished, I stooped to collect mother of pearl shells that smelt of salt and time, not knowing that in just months I'd be stooping to lay baby tears on the rectangle of lawn that covered your shell. But though you would be a buried shell, I would still smell you.

It's not an especially good photo that one of you on the beach. But the one taken of the five of us at your brother's eighteenth birthday is a beauty. Your smile is wide, though it's hard to see into your deep, brown eyes. There we are, the five of us like Siamese quins shouldered together. And yet, and yet, I sense you're hovering.

These last few weeks when I am becalmed by the stillness of your death, I sift through your still life, wishing you were smiling in this one or that your eyes weren't red from the flash, annoyed you were so camera shy. When I find what fits, the stillness goes, replaced by anxiety as I tell the girl in the shop how big I want it, and 'I won't lose any definition, will I?' 'Show me exactly what size he'll be then.' She must know I've lost you, the girl in the shop, for I've become a regular customer. 'Thirty minutes', she says. 'Come back in thirty minutes.' I sit on the bench outside the shop, trying not to stare at the girl as she answers the phone and serves other customers when she should be concentrating on your image.

My husband doesn't like me banging holes in the plaster, so I've removed the large watercolour that hung on the brick wall. A gallery of still-lives now fills that brick wall that meets a cathedral ceiling. I offer yet another badge to the memorial, stand back and stare, aware how each time the stillness takes a hold of me, your photo's bigger than the last one. At this rate the shrine will run out of space.

The stillness within me lasts too short a time. As it fades the flailing fist inside my chest takes over. If, momentarily, the flailing stops, the pulsing pain of bitten-down quicks remind me.

The cemetery trustees have sent me the paperwork requesting the words that are to be inscribed on your plaque. Sixteen words that must encapsulate your life's meaning. All my energy is focused on composing those meagre lines. I walk the brick paths that surround my house, aware of the weeds that have sprung up since your death. The annuals have wilted. I don't think even the perennials will survive.

So many words I want the world to remember you by. If I was asked to name but one, it would be your loyalty. Your downfall really, for if you hadn't had this characteristic, impregnable as the steel rod in your right leg, you would have been able to shrug off your girlfriend dishonouring you. I must be careful. Must string words together for the plaque that will honour you and not words that will help assuage my guilt.

I know a man whose mother died just weeks ago. He was a good son to his mother. He hasn't stopped crying. I have no pity for him, for his tears are for himself…' I wasn't patient enough, wasn't understanding of her frailty, was too quick to get angry at her foolishness.' He cries because he wanted to have her a bit longer.

Real grief is when those left behind cry because the one who has died has taken a large measure of beauty with them.

It cuts so deep. Yes, my son, it cuts so deep.

Chapter 5

I'd gone to bed after tying helium balloons to kitchen chairs. The table was set with a clown theme of party hats, serviettes, whistles, and disposable plates. In the darkness, I mentally walked through what needed to be done first thing in the morning; defrost party pies, put finishing touches on the cake that resembled a cricket oval, wrap Pass the Parcel presents, put a rinse in my hair, then…

I answered the phone on the third ring.

'There's a Telecom van on the oval,' you screamed down the line. 'They're watching me!'

'Huh?'

'There've been watching me for weeks now, videoing me through the dark window.'

I cranked myself up on an elbow. 'What're you talking about?'

'Gotta go, the line's bugged.'

I called your name, but you were gone. Had you been smoking that stuff again? The line was engaged when I tried to reach you. I hugged myself to stop the shivers. The phone rang again.

'Watch it, Mum. They've got you bugged too.'

'Bugged? Why on earth…?'

'Big things going down, Mum. Big things.'

'Where are you?'

'At Dad's.'

'Is he there?'

'Nah. Nah. Fishing up the Murray. That bloody van's still

here.' I heard the venetian slats being parted. Imagined you peering into the dark. 'They've been there two weeks now. Pretending to dig up the oval. Pretending to go home at night.'

'Listen Darling…'

'Don't phone me. It's safer if I call you.'

I again tried to ring you back. Again I shivered in the dark.

'What's going on?' My husband groggily surfaced from a deep sleep. In stops and starts I paraphrased what you'd been saying. He put an arm around my shoulders as if his weight could stop my trembling. 'I'll answer it next time,' he said. But next time you wouldn't speak to anyone but me. Over the next few hours, only when you thought it was safe to talk, your skewed thoughts shot up the line, smacking me in the mouth.

'What the hell's he been taking?' said my husband, anger overriding his confusion.

'It'll be okay. You go back to sleep,' I said. 'Useless both of us sitting up half the night.'

I left my bed and sat in front of the gaping hearth. Rocked myself for comfort, the phone by my feet. 'What's happening to my boy?' The anchored balloons with their painted smiles and arched eyebrows haughtily stared back at me.

'Listen to me,' I pleaded, answering the phone on the first ring.

'No time for listening. Just action. One step ahead, Mum. That's the agenda now.'

'Listen, I'm coming down.'

'No! Roadblocks. Stay where it's safe. You can't see in the dark.'

'In the morning, then?'

'Yeah, safer when the sun's up.'

'It's too late to cancel the party, I'll be down about one-ish?'

'Be careful.'

Pin the Tail on the Donkey and Pass the Parcel seemed a ludicrous pastime. Eleven boys laughed and screamed and had pretend punch-ups and stuffed themselves stupid. One even spewed on the new rug. The house looked like Hussein had invaded. I handed out the lolly bags much too early, had each child ready even before his parent rang the doorbell. I left the vomit and ground-in food, left my boys with a neighbour.

As we drove the two hours to your father's house, hardly a word was spoken, my thoughts swamped by feelings I was afraid to acknowledge.

You opened the door even before I knocked. You'd lost so much weight. How long since I'd seen you? Only a month, surely. Your face was shadowed and when I kissed you, was surprised to find it freshly shaven. And why the sunglasses? Camouflage?

Before letting us in, you surveyed the street, then closed the door, double checking the lock. You steered us to the bathroom. 'There it is!' You pointed to the ceiling in the shower. I tried so hard to see something. 'I've plugged it up.' You had, for I saw a smear of Polyfilla. 'So lucky. I just happened to look up. That's where they were videoing me.'

I tried to hug you, but you couldn't stand still long enough for me to even do that for you. 'No-one's videoing you, Darling. Anyway, why in the hell would they want to?'

'I know what's up, that's why.'

You went to the kitchen and put the kettle on. Got out mugs and spooned coffee into them. Loaded my mug with sugar, even though I never took sugar. I accepted it though, afraid of unsettling you further.

In the lounge we sipped coffee behind closed blinds. Frantically I searched for something real to ground us all. 'Your brother enjoyed his party. Sends his love.'

'Right. Good.' Your eyes darted at the ceiling. I've been trying to catch that motherfucker all night.' I looked but couldn't see anything. You put down the mug. Rolled the TV guide and jumped onto the couch. It's a fucking IRA terrorist,' you said, hitting the ceiling with the rolled paper.

I closed my mouth, afraid I'd start laughing and never stop. I wanted to say, 'You're bloody mad!', like I would in normal circumstances, but was frightened the label might stick. You squashed the fly against the dramas yet to be played out on the telly. Its death seemed to calm you.

As if it was just a normal afternoon entertaining your mother and stepfather, you sat on the couch and reached beneath the coffee table. An album is what you opened, the one I'd put together. The time when there was just us two. 'Remember this?' you said, pointing to a shot of us spread-eagled on a tartan blanket. I nodded. 'And this? And this? And this?'

'Of course. Of course. I remember everything.'

Over the next hour you were as rational as the sun that rises and sets. No crazy mutterings, no hidden agendas to wade through. Even so, as dusk began to fall, I asked you to come home with us. You gave an emphatic, 'No.'

'What will you do tonight, then?'

'Get a pizza, watch a video.'

'Here my shout.' I gave you twenty dollars.

As you walked us to the car, I tried not to stare at the Telecom van on the oval. 'Ring me tonight then. Okay? I'll be home all night.'

Distracted, you nodded, then reached to pick up a rock from the gutter. 'This shouldn't be here!' Affronted, you went back inside cradling the rock. Before starting the engine we sat stunned in the warm interior where doors kept everything out.

The drive home was as silent as the drive down. This time, with our confusion there was a real fear we couldn't name. Easier to pretend everything would be all right. Must've been that stuff you smoke.

The boys were worn out from partying and swimming in the neighbour's pool. At home, left-over balloons had drifted up to the ceiling. My husband supervised the boys' bedtime while I cleaned up the dried vomit and ground-in cake.

I kept checking the time, then the phone to make sure it was working.

'Come to bed, it's ten already. Get some sleep,' said my husband, taking the mop from my hand. I did as I was told. It was twenty-four hours since I'd really slept.

I dreamt a carrier pigeon was caught in a trap. Its squeals woke me. I answered the phone on the second ring.

Silence.

'Is that you, Darling?'

'Trim your words, Mum. Don't give 'em too much.'

'Look, stop this! There's no-one listening in. I'm dullsville, not a bloody terrorist!'

Silence.

'And where've you been, you promised to ring earlier?'

'It's safer at night. Roadblocks are down.'

'Have you eaten?'

'Yeah. Yeah. Now listen carefully. The CIA are onto us. It was Jack Nicholson…

'Wha…'

'Stop interrupting. I've only got sixty seconds before a trace. Jack Nicholson, you know in *One Flew Over…*'

'…*The Cuckoo's Nest.*'

'Yeah, well, he wasn't all he was cracked up to be.'

'Listen!' I'm screaming and so tone down my voice, afraid of scaring him away. 'I'm coming down.'

'No. Stay put! You can't get in. I've boarded up the doors and windows. Gotta go.'

On the half hour throughout the night I listened as you relayed how the KGB were infiltrating the water pipes and that you had a cache of arms buried in the backyard and a bazooka under the bed. If anyone tries to take you they're mincemeat.

The sun rose as I sat huddled in the huge armchair, the phone beside me. But this time, I'd taken the handset off the cradle, temporarily placing you out of reach. Need time to think.

Words, thoughts, feelings eddied. I'm being sucked into a whirlpool. What to do? I could wake my husband who sleeps unaware of the ongoing trauma, could ring my brothers, the two I could always rely on. But I felt my beautiful, sick son was my problem.

What to do, what to do? Should I believe my gentle giant has a cache of arms? I jumped at the pipes when they creaked, imagined little fur hats squeezing from the taps. In the greyness of dawn, sleepless, mad with fear, I'm a drifting island. Floating, floating towards the sun's warmth. But, no! I'm not a drifting island. I'm his mother! I put the receiver back in the cradle and the phone immediately shrilled.

'If you love me, really love me, then you'll bring a packet of cigarettes down!'

'But how will I get in if you've barricaded the doors and windows?'

'Put them in the letterbox.'

'No. I can't.' I'm afraid. Of my son? Yes.

'If you don't, then I'll blow my head off.'

Moaning, I disconnected you, unable anymore to witness your disintegration. No longer could I deny how deep your illness had dug at your soul.

Without hesitating, for I knew if I did I could lose you forever, I dialled 000 and asked for the police.

I gave the woman constable my name and address and phone number, as if I was intoning an affirmation; I took her through the events of the last two days. I got to the part about the bazooka when the line was disconnected. Immediately, I called back. A different voice this time, male, sounding even younger than the constable before. Calmly I tried to get him to understand the disintegration that was happening when I heard:

'Just hang up. It's that woman from Mont Park again.'

Suddenly, dial tone.

Shocked, I sat there. Outside birdsong volleyed from tree to tree. Inside I vacillated from wanting to hide in the broom cupboard, to persisting for your sake.

How long was the phone silent? An hour? Two hours? The next time I answered, it was your father home from his fishing trip. 'What the fuck's going on? Everything's boarded up. A circle of candles. Hole punched in the wall. My home brew's been sucked dry. Where's he gone? Is he in a cult or something?'

'Yes, yes, it must be a cult!' Any straw would do.

'Fuckin' hell.'

'He must be sick, too. Yes, sick. Needs a rest in hospital.' We try to negotiate a way of dealing with all this. We'll ring each other once we hear from you.

No sooner had I hung up than the phone cracked into life again.

'Mum. I'm on my way. Start boarding up the windows. Lever the beds and tables against the doors. Block the heating ducts and cement the taps.'

'Yes, all right. I will. Call me from the station and I'll pick you up.' I'm so frightened. For you. For me. For us all.

It must have been only minutes, but my feelings stretched to hours as I sat in the study holding the phone, hating what I must do.

I held the fridge magnet with the number I'd never had to ring. I tell the local police my son thinks a fly is an IRA terrorist, Telecom are filming him and the KGB are in the plumbing, and he says he has a bazooka. 'Has he been taking drugs?' asked the official voice. I don't know. Perhaps. Probably. I don't know. The official voice told me what to do.

My husband tried to make the day as normal for the boys as possible. They knew nothing of what was happening to the brother they adored. For over two hours I stayed in the study, away from the curious gaze of my children. My husband brought me cups of tea and toast, concerned at my pallor, my chattering teeth. He put the portable heater right up against me. Still I was cold. 'Please don't come to me,' I whispered over and over. But of course you did, for I am your mother. The one person you can always trust, no matter what.

When the phone rang I couldn't bring myself to answer. It was my husband who handed me the phone.

'Mum, I'm here at the station. I'm waiting for you. Don't be long!'

'Stay put. I'll be there in five minutes.'

My husband dialled the police, and handed me the phone. I cried as I surrendered your trust in me.

I was taken to the interview rooms located in the basement. There you were. I sat beside you. Your eyes darted around me, above me. Lips outlined in black, making you look demonic. Vanilla essence you told me, you'd run out of grog.

'Watch it, Mum, they're filming you.'

'No, they're not.'

You pointed upwards. This time there was a security camera in the ceiling. Suddenly you upended the desk and barricaded us into the room. Into safety, you told me. My mouth hung open, empty of words. Two policemen battled their way in, then charged at you. I backed out, heard one of them say, 'Careful, don't break his arm.'

'Nooo,' you moaned as I heard the click, click of handcuffs. For your own protection, I presumed.

'JUDAS MOTHER!' you screamed.

They separated us then. And so to stay focused, I took a scrap of paper from my handbag and scribbled…potatoes, rice, peanut butter, cereal, Vegemite, Judas Mother, JUDAS MOTHER, JUDAS MOTHER. Images flooded of my beautiful new born-son, bloodied and mucous-streaked, your mouth already searching.

When the Police Surgeon finally arrived to certify you, my shopping list was long enough to sustain two years in a fallout shelter.

Chapter 6

Behind the high brick walls, I waited for you. The people who lived here shuffled from room to room like a disjointed Conga line, all locked into a nightmare where few could enter. I tried not to stare at the ones who retraced their step, talked to themselves, or stared suspiciously at me. A woman in a stained tracksuit, handbag regally carried, approached me. 'How do you do, Madam? My name is Dame Wilhelmina.'

I shook her hand, said how nice it was to meet her.

'Have you seen my parrot? "I've got a secret," it says. 'I've got a secret. I've got a secret, I've…" '

'No, I haven't.'

'I'm so worried about it. I'm all it has. So worried.' From her handbag she produced a wrinkled, black and white photo of a caged parrot. A little girl of about five stood beside the cage. I could see the resemblance to the girl in the photo in the way Dame Wilhelmina held her head to one side.

'How old is your parrot?'

'As old as my secret. My daddy gave it to me for keeping secrets. Do you have secrets? No, I can tell you don't!' She sneered, grabbed back the photo. 'Well, my daddy loved me!' She went off to introduce herself to another visitor who had just been admitted to the foyer.

If it weren't for the high brick walls, and deadlocked door, I could be waiting for a friend in the foyer of a hotel, a luncheon date. But this hotel warrants only two stars with its worn carpet and desolate air.

It's been two days since I've seen you, two days since you called me 'Judas Mother'. 'Tell her not to visit me', you told your psychiatrist, who in turn, told me to wait until you wanted me to come. Last night, just as I was heading off to bed, you phoned to tell me you shouldn't be in a place like this, and how could I be so cruel. I asked if there was anything you wanted. 'Yeah, cigarettes and my Walkman. Could you bring them in?'

Tired of waiting with the other apprehensive looking visitors, I went in search of you, found you in the recreation room, waiting for a turn at the coloured balls. You were unaware of me as I watched from the doorway. You looked so gaunt. Your face still had the shadowed look, reminding me of the time I snuck a look at a partial eclipse of the sun. You noticed me hovering, and hesitantly came to me. I tilted my face to kiss you. 'You've shaved your hair off.' I rubbed your globe-like head.

'Had to, to get rid of the bugs.'

Lice or transmitters, I wondered as balls clicked and missed.

'I've bought you some grapes and cigarettes.' As if proof was needed, I opened the paper bag, but your focus was on the cue stick. You laid it on the floor, first pointing it towards the window, then realigning it so the stick pointed to the farthest wall. We all need a compass of sorts, I reasoned, gulping anxiety. I followed you to the room with the TV where only Homer Simpson acted zany. Our knees barely touched as we sat on the couch in the stifling heat.

'I need a beanie. It's cold in here.'

'I'll bring one in tomorrow.'

'They want me to take medication.'

'It might help to…'

'They can stick it! There's nothing wrong with me.' You stared at my mouth, defying me to say otherwise.

You looked so lost, alone, and, although you didn't ask, I said your stepfather had a meeting today but would be in tomorrow. My husband hadn't told me anything of the sort, in fact, we hadn't yet discussed how we'd juggle the visits so you could have one of us visit during the day, one in the evening. I just wanted to reassure you of our ongoing love.

'No! I don't want anyone to see me here. Especially the boys. Don't bring them in. Not like this!' You jumped up as if you had someplace else to go. Slowly, so as not to alarm you, I stood and hugged you still, but I doubt you felt me.

'Go now before they lock you in too.'

Outside the building with its barred windows, I sat in the car. The dense silence wrapped me so tightly, I could hardly breathe. I wound down the window, listened for sound, anything that would tell me I was still alive.

Somehow, as if in slow motion, I managed to drive past pedestrians and houses and light poles. I stopped at a green light. There was a screeching of brakes behind me. 'What's up, lady! You waitin' for the right shade of green or somethin'?'

Across the way, a man threw open the door of a delivery truck and unloaded wreaths onto the church steps. I ran from the car, not heeding the blasting horns. I ran into the bluestone building, my feet pounding down the aisle to confront the statue with the long, sad face. Why was I here, when I didn't believe? 'My son is lost too,' shouted my echoing voice. I struck out at the marble woman who grieved forever, but it was me who fell to the floor weeping, listing motherly, commonplace sins on the slate in my head, just as I'd once written the complaints of my childhood in the mist on the louvred window. This time, though, the list would not evaporate in the sun's warmth.

The confessional door opened and, not wanting intrusion, I grabbed the radio that had fallen from my bag, and plugged my ears with the earphones. Listening to heavy metal in that sacrosanct place, I didn't at first feel the tentative touch of hands crippled from arthritis. A woman mouthed words at me. I pulled the plugs from my ears.

'Is there anything I can do, love?' she said.

'I forgot to give this to my son when I visited him and now he's got no-one to listen to.' I cupped the radio, just as I'd once supported your head in the bath.

'Sick, is he?'

'Very.'

'I'll say a prayer for him then.' The woman's shoes had been cut at the front to make room for bulging corns that looked like peanut shells. 'It's marvellous what they can do with modern technology these days, love.'

Yes, I thought. That's if you've got a dickey heart, or an arm that needs re-attaching, or a virus that needs a name. I plugged myself back into heavy metal, preferring that to the old woman's platitudes.

When I arrived home, my husband was slouched in a chair watching the telly. He didn't look at me when I greeted him. I sat beside him, aware of how his weak chin was becoming even more pronounced. 'How much of our life do you reckon we spend at traffic lights?' I said.

He gave me a confused look.

'It must be a year or two that we just sit there waiting for the lights to change.'

'Never thought about it,' he said, then, 'How is he?'

'Ratshit.'

He closed his eyes tight as though something gruesome was on the screen. It was only a weatherman. He hadn't eaten so I went to the kitchen to put something together.

When the weatherman had announced the sun and storms for the next seven days, my husband came into the kitchen to boil the kettle.

'It's not so bad you know,' I said. 'It's a hospital atmosphere. People just more spaced out, that's all.' I watched as he added cold milk to the coffee before adding water. A new fetish. He said adding milk first prevented the coffee from getting burnt.

'Thought you could visit first thing tomorrow, then I'll go in the evening. He doesn't want anyone to see him like he is, but I thought if you only stayed a few minutes, just to let him know you care.' I prattled on, my husband's lack of enthusiasm making me anxious.

'I'm ah, going into hospital myself tomorrow,' he said, and, mistaking my look of astonishment for concern, added, 'just for the day.'

'What?'

'I'm ah, going to have my nose done.' I stared, confused while he looked embarrassed. 'Simple procedure really. Straightening the bone in my nose will help alleviate this bloody sinus, and it could work in your favour too.' He gave me a wary smile. 'Might improve the snoring and…' I watched his tongue flapping and wanted to impale it on the fork. He dunked a teddy biscuit and I laughed when its head fell onto his tie, laughed till I was out of breath.

'You're going to have a…a…repair job done! My son's in a mental hospital and you're going in for a tune-up!'

'It's been booked for months.'

'Bloody cancel it!' I pushed my plate aside and the poached eggs slid onto the table looking as goggle-eyed as I was.

'Look, I'll visit him when I'm over it. The bruising should go down in a couple of days.'

'You're a gutless wonder!'

'You don't understand…'

'And don't give me that shit about your grandmother and how you were forced to visit her every Sunday when she locked herself out of her mind. You were a kid then!' I stormed out of the room, but not before adding, 'While you're at it, find out how much a ball transplant costs.'

In bed, I pretended to read while he undressed. He sat on the bed, shaking his socks right side out, shaking the bed.

'Look, sweetie, I know you need support, but if you cancel on the same day you lose the deposit. And I'm sure…'

As he justified himself, all I could think about was the gap in his front teeth had widened even further, a perfect parting.

'…and I've already paid a thousand upfront.' He tossed the shirt into the laundry basket.

The book I pretended to read hit the far wall and pages scattered from the broken spine. 'You are so frigging cheap! Cheap! Cheap! Cheap!'

'Keep your voice down. You sound like a distressed chook.'

I kicked the doona off, knelt on the bed, nose nearly pressing on his dysfunctional one. 'So frigging cheap you won't even donate your organs. Well, you know what? When you die I'm going to donate your heart, lungs, eyes, kidney, liver, and…and…the whole fucking kit and caboodle.'

'Come on, this isn't about me. You're upset because…'

'And when I get you back as ashes, know what I'm going to do?'

'Probably give me a good blow-job,' he said, stifling a laugh. 'Now keep your voice down.' He closed his eyes, hugged the sheet to him like I was a bad draught.

'Keep my voice down?' I opened the window wide, then shouted, 'As the world turns, my son slips off the edge while my husband gets to breathe easier!'

'Wake me when the alarm goes off,' he said, grabbing a pillow.

I counted how many loud steps it took him to reach the spare bedroom. Eighteen.

I woke to a bird whistling a melody, a prolonged wolf whistle. The alarm buzzed. I softy walked twenty-one steps to the bedroom where my husband slept. Lightly, I tapped on the door, not caring if he heard or not. My head felt like it'd been scalped, the skin stretched over a throbbing drum. The only thing I had to be grateful for that morning was the boys were away on a Scout camp and so didn't witness what had gone on the previous evening.

When he came in to get dressed, I was back in bed. He kicked the wardrobe door closed, snapped his tie as he knotted it, jangled coins for parking, repeatedly clicked his briefcase as he checked he had everything. It sounded like a bloody railway station – change being given, doors slamming, commuters opening briefcases. But wasn't that what our bedroom had become like over the last few years? A railway station where regular derailments occurred and where we rushed past each other, occasionally coupling on to shunt off again. I buried my head beneath the pillow to stifle my giggles at the nonsensical rhyme that popped into my head. Occasional roots instead of toots.

'What're you laughing at?'

'Nothing much.'

'Sometimes, I think you're losing it, too.'

'Like mother, like son, you mean?'

'Sorry. Bad choice of words.'

Even when he was at the other end of the house, I could hear him, the way he slammed the fridge door, the door he'd only recently told me to be careful with as the rubber seal was starting to rot. Then the front door slammed.

I showered, made an effort to get dressed, but my vision blurred. The stretched pigskin that was my scalp, amplified the thumping of the angry drummer. Before the migraine tablets put me to sleep, I phoned the hospital, told them I was too ill to visit. Then I phoned work.

Whenever my husband was late home I'd imagine him in a car accident. And while waiting for the knock on the door, I'd mentally go through my wardrobe selecting what to wear at his funeral. How brave I'd be till the mourners left, breaking down only when I hugged his empty dressing gown. But this night I planned food for the wake and the trips I'd take on his superannuation.

I rang the hospital. You'd had an uneventful day. Still refusing to take medication.

When my husband arrived home he looked like he'd been mugged, face bruised and swollen, and up his nose two white plugs streaked with blood, reminding me of how the orifices of the dead are corked. I sucked my lips to stop from laughing at the spectacle he made. Wondered what was in the box he so carefully held.

'You look sore,' I said.

'You don't look so hot yourself.'

'I've been zonked out all day. Bloody migraine again.'

'Here, this is for you.' He placed the box on the table.

'What is it?'

'Something I think you've been missing.'

The string was tightly knotted, and there were holes in the top of the box. Inside, curled around each other were two kittens, one tabby, one ginger. Momentarily I forgot everything, even the wake and overseas trips I'd been planning just minutes before.

'Lucky's been gone over a year now. Time you replaced him.'

I'd thought I was doing the right thing for Lucky who was so unlucky. I'd taken him to the vet because of his bad breath. He died from cardiac arrest as the rotten tooth was being pulled.

'What're you going to call them?' he asked.

'Grey Cat and Ginger.'

'Original.'

'How'd you manage all this?'

'Picked them up before my appointment. Got the vet to knock them out a bit.'

I smiled my thanks at his swollen eyes that seemed frozen in a lewd blink. 'Did it hurt?'

'They were out to it before they knew it.'

'No. Your nose. Did it hurt?'

He patted the bandage. 'It'll be worth it, I hope.'

'You never mentioned it before…the fact that you didn't like yourself the way you were.'

He shrugged me off. The cats stirred, took in their surroundings. Suddenly I felt an unfamiliar attachment to my husband, and wanted to show him how grateful I was. But the picture of my son alone, surrounded by misfits, got in the way.

'I didn't get to the hospital today. Spoke to his nurse though.'

'And?'

'Still off the beam. They reckon it could be a while. First hurdle is to get him to admit he's sick and then voluntarily take the medication. After that, it'll be a juggling process with the pills till they get it right.'

'I'll pop in and see him as soon as the swelling goes down. Only scare him witless looking like this.'

'No.'

'No?'

'Like I said last night, he doesn't want you or the boys to see him in there. Best we respect that.'

'He'll change his mind in a couple of days.'

'I'm sorry about last night. It's just…I feel like a shanghai stretched as far as it'll go.'

'I can imagine.'

No you can't imagine, I nearly said. It's not your son who's lost his anchor, who's been shipwrecked on an alien coast. I knew that by not sharing my feelings with my husband I was not only short-changing him, but myself. Growing up in a household with five brothers, I'd so often heard the catch-phrase, Big boys don't cry, that I'd become one of the boys. A stiff upper lip only served to imprison feelings, feelings that sometimes escaped, cloaked in an unrealistic anger.

'Why didn't you tell me you weren't happy with your nose?'

'It's just a nose,' he said and kissed me on the cheek and went off to bed. Alone with the kittens, I wished it could be like it once was. Kissing, chewing on each other's lips. All we ever gave each other now was a cursory kiss, from habit more than anything. His always felt like a wet postage stamp. I wondered what mine felt like.

When I finally turned in, my husband, his nose free of the plugs, was snoring. The irony of it all didn't escape me. My husband reinventing himself, while my son shaved his hair off, exposing his nakedness. I climbed into bed, spooned my body into my husband's, grateful for the warmth.

Next morning, persistent miaowing got me moving. The kittens, ears alert, were at the glass door, staring at the windy day. Hesitantly, they followed me into the grey morning, licked up the milk and cereal I offered. Satisfied, they began to explore the backyard. Wind skittered leaves across the patio. Grey Cat jumped onto the garden seat, then the barbeque, to escape them. Ginger, eyes wide, joined Grey Cat in the safety of height. Becoming used to the moving leaves, they jumped down to stalk a snail that took cover in its shell. Grey Cat soon lost interest in the snail when she discovered a grasshopper. She trapped it in her mouth, lay it on its back at my feet, trophy-like. I cupped the grasshopper and set it free, high up on the grapevine.

Suddenly, I couldn't wait to see you. The kittens had crapped on the kitchen floor. I was in too much of a hurry to clean it up.

Chapter 7

The photos in the collage your brothers made have been put back in the albums. Casserole dishes and platters have all been returned, and the last of the flowers have been tossed onto the compost. The doorbell hardly rings now the novelty of your death has worn off.

I am reminded of when I left your father and set up home for just you and me. Most of my friends ostracised me, not that they didn't hurriedly drop in on the way to somewhere else, but I was exiled to that safe place where freed-up women are out of reach of husbands and boyfriends.

This time I've been banished to another safe place where friends and family keep their distance. It's as if they can only be in the presence of such raw grief for a limited time. When I mention you there is silence. Embarrassed, pitying, I-don't-know-what-to-say, silence. Can't they understand that if I don't articulate my memories I'll go mad? By saying your name I dredge the wonderful, foolhardy, inane, funny, weird things you said and did. Your name is the springboard from which I dive, only to surface when I'm replenished by your memory.

Yesterday, a tidal wave slammed into my gut. I crawled into bed, pulled the doona over my head, and waited for the excess of grief to ebb. But this will never happen all the while I think of you. Only when I have to focus on going from A to B, doing 1, 2, and 3, does the fog in my head clear enough for me to see.

If I were an artist I would paint every fleeting, lingering image of you for the world to remember. My vision can be full of people and colour, yet they become muted when you appear in my mind's canvas. I have a still-life of you walking past the kitchen window, stooped from the weight of your backpack (always the clink of bottles of beer), carrying a fishing rod, and collapsible stool. The rod and stool were the sum of your possessions, the only things you never lost, gave away, or traded in at Cash Converters. In fact, your life was one of loss and conversion, changing roles as often as your clothes. Son / stepson, rational / irrational.

Today tears roll out, stinging as if in self-flagellation. I lie on my bed, see the sun still shines while the cat miaows and the potatoes burn, and I want to leave all this, to go in search of you, just to stand beside you my towering son, if only for a minute. And if I could see you were safe and a constant warmth embraced you, I would gladly return to all this. But if you were trembling, well then I'd stay with you and start at the beginning when there was just you and I.

'Dinner's ready,' calls my husband. I can smell burnt toast.

'We're coming.' I close my journal. And though only I walk down the hall (the words about you clutched to my chest), I think nothing odd about answering 'we' instead of 'I', for wherever I go you are with me, weighting me with your death, elevating my spirit for having known you.

'What are you writing?' he asks.

'Just stuff.'

'About…?'

'Thoughts, feelings.'

'Oh, right.' He looks outside. 'Do you want to see a movie tonight?'

'Not really.'

'Stay home then?'

I shrug. It doesn't matter if I'm home, or out. Wherever I am, my husband is unable to reach me in my distress. It's safer for him to stay at arm's length. My guess is he's afraid if he does mention you, feelings might ignite leading to questions, answers even, that best remain buried. So marooned I remain, not even dots or dashes can alert him to my distress. I sit on my island waiting for a king tide to carry me to that place that must exist, a place where I'll be weightless from the joy of sharing sorrow.

He ladles soup into four bowls. 'Chicken soup,' he says, 'food for the soul.'

I am neither hungry, nor full, thirsty or sated, only skewered.

I want you back, rigid in the leather chair, pretending to shrug off the kisses I planted when I said goodnight.

As I eat the soup and burnt toast, I look at my family, what is left of my family, and wonder what they are thinking. After our evening meal now, we tend to find a corner where we sit alone with a newspaper, book, television, even silence, disguising our thoughts. Tonight is no exception.

My husband is in the lounge reading the *Financial Review*. I perch on the arm of his chair. He doesn't seem to notice me until I touch his shoulder. 'How are you coping?' I ask.

His gaze is fixed on the headline, 'Inflation at an All-Time High'. 'I have so many regrets,' he says.

I wait for him to continue, but he doesn't fill me in. 'I've decided to get some help. See a counsellor,' I say. 'Do you want to come with me?' I know what his answer will be. He thinks counselling is a bit like a confessional. A cop-out. In the end, you have only yourself to answer to, he once told me.

'No, I'll be fine.'

'Sometimes you need someone to help you find the questions before you can be answerable,' I say. He still stares at the same headline.

I find my middle son stretched out on his bed. He looks Mickey Mouse-like with the headphones that fill his head with music.

'How's it going?' I ask. He removes the headphones, makes room for me to lie down beside him.

'I've been exempted from the uni exams.'

'Good.' I recognise Pearl Jam through the headphones. On the wall is a framed collage of that band's record covers. On the desk is a picture of my three sons, the youngest with two front teeth missing. 'What I meant was, how are you going?'

'Yeah. Okay.'

'Do you need to talk?'

He looks at me as though I'm the one who needs to talk.

'It's okay to talk about him, you know.'

'I do talk about him. With my mates.'

'I need to get a few things off my chest,' I say.

He looks at me, afraid. Afraid I'll unburden myself on him?

'I'm going to see a counsellor. Do you need to?'

'No, I'm okay.'

'Will you let me know if you're not?'

'Sure. 'Night, Mum.'

I find my youngest in the study, downloading music onto a disc.

'Is that legal?' I ask.

He shrugs. 'Everyone's doing it.'

'Well, that would make it legal then.' I laugh, but he doesn't get my drift.

I pull up a chair and try to concentrate as he shows me how to copy music. As he clicks the cursor, here, there and everywhere – too fast for me to keep up, he says, 'I really miss my big bro.'

I put my arm around him. 'I know.' Then after a while I say, 'I'm going to have some counselling to help me get through this.'

'How will that help?'

'A counsellor will get me talking. Get me to spill out stuff that otherwise might stay stuck and end up tripping me down the track.'

The computer pings, and the disc slides out. 'Can I come with you?'

Within two weeks we are at the church where the local counselling service operates. At reception, we flip through dated

Reader's Digests, and torn National Geographics. Background music of bird and water sounds make me aware of how full my bladder is. When I return from the toilet, the counsellor is shaking your brother's hand and I observe how confident he is, how he looks her straight in the eyes. You often found it difficult meeting others' eyes…but inevitably, that crooked smile.

She leads us into the office, indicates seating, closes the door, settles herself beside us. 'So, what are we here for?'

She must know why. The secretary made a point of finding out the reason when I made the appointment. Perhaps it's part of the routine, getting us to state the obvious. So I go through my usual spiel – I've got it down pat now – simple, straightforward facts. No embellishment needed. For dramatic effect, your deed stands alone.

For the next forty-five minutes, your brother, with only the gentlest of prods, talks non-stop about you. I try to absorb everything he says, but get lost in the telling, so remnants are all I remember. Though anything but remnants they are!

The hardest part is I never got to say goodbye.
And life wasn't fair to him.
He didn't have the opportunities we had.
His father didn't care about him much.
He didn't do well at school.
Didn't have a job.
We were the fortunate ones.
He missed out on so much.

Tears drip onto his clasped hands.

'I think he is a very lucky man having a brother who loves him so much,' says the counsellor, and I want to hug her for using the present tense.

'He was a good brother. He always looked out for me. When he could.'

Towards the end of the session, he looks to me. 'Did you want to say anything, Mum?'

I shake my head. 'I'll have my turn when you've run out of words. There's no hurry for me.' No, for he is the one who will bear the scar longer than me. At least, I hope he will.

Driving home, he says, 'I liked her.'

'And I like you!' I say, chucking him under the chin.

So many houses, front rooms lit up like beacons. As I steer the car along main roads I stare, try to catch a glimpse inside of people leading ordinary lives. My fear that your death would somehow untie our family is replaced with the thought it might unite us even more. I taught you that, didn't I? Even with the worst scenario, you can find a positive. I didn't teach you well enough.

That night in bed, I say to my husband, 'You said a few weeks ago you had regrets. What are they?'

A deep intake of breath, and then, 'It's hard enough me knowing them without putting them out there. Anyway, you've got enough stuff to deal with.'

Three weeks later I go alone for counselling. My son has decided he's run out of words. I sit there in my red suit, a carry-over from my corporate days. Red power suit, yet feeling powerless.

'How are?' she says.

'I feel like I'm sleepwalking with my eyes open.'

'That sounds a scary feeling.'

'There's the deepest stillness in me. See, he was the tide that pushed and pulled me, the tide that kept me anchored, and I was his shore.'

She pushes the box of Kleenex towards me, but I'm not crying. I don't think.

'It's like I've become two people. The one everyone's always known…in control, on top of things. And then there's the other me, so passionately sad, unable to find a reason for getting out of bed. You know, I've got to the stage where I envy my cats. I just want to get down on all fours and wind into myself and let the sun warm me forever.'

'Sounds safe,' she says.

'It's the looking back that knocks me for six.'

'How do you mean?'

'When I was a kid, the old woman who lived across the road taught me a few safety rules. One was, when out, always drink from the left side of a cup because most people are right-handed and I wouldn't get germs that way. Another was to never sit on a toilet other than your own. So when using public toilets, I stand like a man, but backwards. She was full of homilies too, this old woman. The one that's stayed with me all these years is, "Look back but don't stare".'

'Right,' she says, but I can tell she's not on my wavelength.

'See, how can I not stare? How can I not reach for those feelings I can no longer embrace. Not ever. His broad back, long arms, brown eyes, and his melt-in-the-mouth sausage rolls. Only if I stare can I truly feel.'

'It's important to feel. As difficult as it can be.'

'Yes, but why can't I show my feelings?'

'You are now.'

'No, I'm telling them! It's like my heart and mind operate independent of each other. You know, I practice trying to show my sorrow. I stand in front of the mirror rehearsing, practicing the words that usually flow so matter-of-fact. Words…as if just placing a grocery order. Now, I tell myself, force a tear, a sob, try to make the words catch on barbed wire. My son is dead. See! Simple as adding string beans to the shopping list. Still I practice, for I've never bought string beans.'

'As a kid were you taught not to cry?'

'I tried to be one of the boys.'

'And big boys don't cry,' she says.

'You grew up with brothers, too,' I say, but, typically, she moves the conversation back to me.

I leave the session still feeling powerless.

Next stop is the hairdresser. First haircut since you left us. She sits behind me on a stool with stilled castors. Her mouth agape, scissors silent, as she hears what I have to say. Of how the noose was your plaited trackie pants. Swollen tongue, pacific blue. When I'm finished staring back, it's she who sighs, she who holds a mirror behind my head so I can still see backwards.

When I arrive home, everyone is in bed sleeping. I give my teeth a quick scrub and also turn in for the night. Again, the silence keeps me awake. So often I can be on the edge of sleep when I hear gasps as imagery invades the stillness…

Chipped ashtray; wiped clean. Empty brandy bottle; in the bin. Wallet; on the kitchen table. The note beneath…

Useless to try to sleep when memory gets a stranglehold.

Again, the sentry's alert to my night movements.

'Mum?'

I turn on the hall light.

'I thought you'd be asleep by now,' I say, rubbing my fingers through his hair stiff with gel.

'I miss him so much.'

'I had a dream about him the other night,' I say.

'Tell me.'

'Well, I was outside in the garden weeding, and I sensed someone was behind the gate. When I looked, there he was, peering in through the slats. He gave me a pair of socks, they were stolen, and a candelabra. Five candles in all.'

'Strange dream.'

'Yeah.'

'Did he look peaceful?'

'Yes. Go to sleep now. I'm just getting a drink.'

I turn off the light, and am halfway to the kitchen when he calls me back.

'What is it?'

'Why don't I dream of him? I want to see him too.'

I lie on the bed, my arm around him. 'You'll dream of him one day.'

'Even if it's just one time. I want to say goodbye.'

I stay beside my weeping son until he is asleep.

In the study I sit at the desk, the lamp spotlighting the unopened letter. 'State Coroner's Office' is printed in the top left-hand corner. I lied, for you didn't look peaceful in my dream. I sensed you were hesitant, as if unsure of how I would greet you. This hurts for always my arms were open for you. But then, as FF pointed out when I told her of the dream, perhaps you were hesitant because you thought I might be angry with you for leaving the way you did. I slit the envelope with the dagger-like opener. 'As requested, find attached the original note left by your son.'

Your childlike scrawl…

I am so very very sorry. Too many to thank. I will see you all in eternity. And to my deepest love, Goodbye. I hope to see you all in eternity. Yours forever. Love forever. Sorry.

Your last words. Or did you curse as you tried to fasten the noose around the bottlebrush?

I stare at those thirty-six words as if beneath, between, is a clue, a sign, that will somehow absolve my guilt.

In my Grandfather's writing case I place your note alongside the last letter my Grandmother wrote to her son, my father, when he was a prisoner-of-war. She died of a brain tumor just weeks before he arrived home. You too were a prisoner, the enemy surrounding, invading your mind, until you surrendered.

I open the file I have made for you. So many statements of interviews to read. Your Nan, friends, mine. Hers, Your Deepest Love, I have sealed in an envelope, along with the letters you wrote her. I'll need distance, a long distance before I can read them.

A man reduced to a file. I have so few tangibles left to show you existed. Rarely did you put pen to paper. No precious letters to me. All I have been able to find is your Nan's recipe you wrote for me – Anzac biscuits. On the back your words: Enjoy these biccies, and don't forget to save some for the soldiers!

I have an astrology book you gave me, paperback, with the inscription:

> For Mum on her 40th birthday
> You don't look a day over 50!
> Your loving son. 1990

That book became my bible for the first few months of my fortieth year, until I realised the book held predictions for 1989. I guessed you purchased it at an Op Shop, or else heavily marked down.

When I return to bed, my husband lies on his back, loudly snoring, arms spread like Jesus. I jab him, tell him to roll over onto his side. Your dream presents. What did they mean? FF thinks he might have been holding an Advent Wreath and not a candelabra. An Advent Wreath, she told me, has five candles, and the fifth is lit on Christmas Eve, a welcoming to eternal life. No, I believe the candles are to light my way. Five candles. You mean, my son, it will get darker still? And the socks? To keep me warm on this cold journey?

Chapter 8

You were watching for me through the window like you did in kinder, except then the door wasn't locked.

I offered my lips. You responded, though with just a whisper-touch of your cheek, eyes still unable to meet mine. I didn't make a big deal about your latest insecurity that made you look like a warrior.

As if afraid of tripping on the geometric patterns on the carpet, you shuffled along, leading the way to the TV room. A midday movie was playing. You seemed entranced as Jeanette McDonald and Nelson Eddy warbled a love song. The thick elastic circling your head stretched as you moved your eyebrows up and down.

I touched you, and your eyebrows bunched together. 'You used to go to bed like that once. Said you were trying to flatten your ears. Remember?'

'They're too big.' You placed gloved hands over your ears stretching them back.

'They're beautiful,' I said, meaning it.

Shrugging, you patted the elastic into place.

You were thirteen when you came to me one night asking me to make a thick elasticised band that would fit around your head. I guessed you wanted to flatten your ears. Every night you wore that band to bed. Sometimes when I came in to kiss you goodnight, and you were already asleep, the band would be twisted and I'd gently take it off. In the morning, when I woke you, it was always back on. You stopped wearing it after a couple of years. Why these six years later have you started wearing it again? Did all this start way back then? The elastic thing…was it really for your ears? Or was there something you were afraid of letting out?

I gave you the old footie beanie from the bag of things I'd brought. You put it on, stretching it over your head. 'C'arn the Bombers,' I said, and you smiled a great big curve as though your team had just kicked a goal.

'Let's go out into the garden,' you said, 'so we can have a cigarette.' You take the one I offer and, without asking, pocket my packet. Your fingers are stained with nicotine. Not much else to do in this place except smoke. People drifted in and out the glass door to where we sat in the secure area. People smoking, pacing, anything to fill in time.

'This is Sylvia.' You introduced me to a woman who could have stepped off a page of *Vogue*.

'I'm getting out today,' she said, a wagging finger emphasising each word.

'That's good.' What else do you say? Hope you stay out, or what put you in here has healed?

'She's in for trying to drown her kid in the bath,' you said, when she went inside. 'The kid's in foster care now.'

'Right,' I said, when everything was wrong. So wrong. It was difficult trying to keep a poker face when I wanted to cry at the sadness in people. But I reined in my feelings for over the last weeks you'd started to let me get closer, though still keeping a safe gap. In case I pulled another stunt like the police surgeon, I supposed.

'And that one over there. She's a weirdo. Don't know what she's in for, but steer clear of her. Had her in high security all last week. Wouldn't turn my back on her.'

As we sat in the garden mulched with cigarette butts, you continued to introduce me to anyone who came outside. I tried hard to make them like me for these people were your extended family, if only temporarily. And if they liked me, they would perhaps treat you well.

'I'm so glad you're taking the medication now.'

'Yeah, well, it's the only way outa here.'

Did you mean you'd stop taking the pills once discharged?

'Dad came in to see me yesterday. Brought me in a couple of stubbies. We're allowed to have one a day, you know.'

'How is he?' I pretended interest. As far as I was aware this was your father's first visit. I couldn't ask you, though, for it would only put you in a position of having to defend him. I was careful never to paint your father the black colour that I saw him. I wanted you to use your own palette.

'Didn't stay long. He reckoned I should hurry up and get out of here, that they're all nut cases.'

'Just as many nuts walking around outside,' I said, unable to help myself.

You laughed, and for an instant I saw your cheeky grin instead of the blank expression – a side effect of the drugs.

I left you then, both of us calm for the first time in weeks.

I had only just got home, having collected your brothers from school, when you rang.

'I've got rights you know!' you screamed.

'Yes, you do,' I said, amazed at how quickly your mood had changed.

'I've rung "A Current Affair".'

'And…?'

'You can't keep someone imprisoned against their will.'

'Sometimes, if it's for their own good, it's…'

'They said they'd interview me. When they have a blank space to fill.'

My heart plummeted at the futility of such a phone call to the local television station, and yet my mind cheered you on for your resilience, for such faith in yourself.

Another week went by. Then one night I'd just arrived home from work and was helping your brother with a school project when you rang me, excited with the news.

'I've lodged an appeal. It's being heard on Friday, I think.'

'What's an appeal entail?'

'I need your support, Mum.'

'Yes, I'll be there.'

'I'm relying on you, Mum.'

'I know you are, Darling. I know.'

'I've gotta get outa here. They've got a contract out on me. Gotta disappear, get into that scheme, you know, where you get a new identity. Gotta get swallowed up.'

I left the school project to ring the hospital. A nurse told me that legally an involuntary patient can be kept in a secure facility for only twenty-eight days. That everyone has the right to appeal for release, though not many have the nous or energy to go through that channel. I was fit to burst, so proud of you. Drugged, confused, and yet you still fought for your rights.

When I returned to the study, your brother had already completed a dossier on you. 'Q: In about 25 words describe each member of your family.' Beneath your name he had written:

My big brother is 6 foot tall, he likes beer and has a nice smile. He doesn't have a job, but he plays cricket with me. He is in hospital but getting better. I wish I could visit him, but he is contagious.

'Who told you he's contagious?'

'My friend at school. She said that was probably why I couldn't visit him.'

'Darling, he's not contagious.'

'Why can't I visit him?'

'Because he thinks the hospital will make you sad.'

'I'm sad not seeing him.'

The day of the appeal I took an early lunch. On the way to the hospital I got a speeding ticket. It wasn't because I was eager to get to the hearing. I was dreading it, dreading what I'd have to say, if asked. No, I was hurrying because I wanted to hold your hand, to support you as best I could.

By now, the staff knew me and unlocked the door without asking for identification. There you were, waiting for me, pacing the foyer. You beamed at me, assuming my support would be to your advantage. A legal-aid solicitor, appointed by the Appeal Panel, was waiting to represent you. He'd asked to meet with me first, and so I was taken to a wood-panelled room with no window, just last year's calendar to break the monotony.

The solicitor didn't stand to greet me, and I realised the alert dog sitting beside him was not just a pet. The solicitor extended his hand and I placed mine in his.

'What will happen,' he said, 'Is that you will probably be asked if you think your son is ready to return to the outside world. As his mother, your opinion will be highly regarded.'

I waited for him to grill me, coach me in what I should say. Instead, he continued to outline the appeal process. I was unable to concentrate, too caught up in my dilemma.

Then hesitantly you entered the wood-panelled room. Wanting to make a positive first impression, you went straight to the solicitor and extended your hand. I swallowed hysterical giggles as the solicitor groped the air, searching for your hand.

'I want to see my file,' you told him, once you'd managed to shake hands. 'I have rights you know. Freedom of Info.'

'Let's first concentrate on how we'll present your appeal.'

'No! I must see my file.'

Nothing would sway you, and so with you leading the way we followed the yellow, arrowed line on the floor that led to the nurse's station. Thirty-eight painted arrows.

'Where is it! I have rights. I want to see my file,' you shouted to the nurse behind the glass screen.

She slid the screen so she could hear you.

'I have rights! My file. Show me my file!'

'I can't do that. There's a formal process that takes about thirty days,' said the nurse. 'Why do you need to see it?'

'ASIO have got it, haven't they!' you said, panicking.

She opened the filing cabinet, took out a file, yours or somebody's – it didn't matter – and solemnly held it up for you to see. I loved that nurse for treating you with such dignity.

'Good. Watch it closely,' you said, temporarily placated.

When it was time for the hearing, we entered a room the size of an army barrack and just as cold. Behind a long table sat the bi-partisan Appeal Committee. The bearded man introduced himself as a psychiatrist who was separate from the workings of the hospital, as was the faded-looking social worker, and the community worker whose soppy eyes reminded me of a cocker spaniel about to be put down. As if attending a court martial, the three of us sat facing the panel. The dog sat to attention. I rewarded it with a pat.

The psychiatrist outlined the reasons we were there. I rested my hand on your leg to stop it jittering, a nervous tremor you inherited from your father. He read from a file, sentences short and unemotional.

'…and so you think you're well enough now to return to the community. Is that right?'

Finally, the accused got to speak. You stood, pushing the chair from beneath you. It scratched the floor like chalk on a blackboard. 'That's right. Sir.'

'Sit down. Relax. We're not that formal here.' The psychiatrist smiled tolerantly until you were seated, then continued with, 'I've got a report from your treating psychiatrist. It gives us some idea of what led up to you being here and it seems…'

'But see, I'd been smoking too much stuff and that tipped me, and the booze didn't help either and…' You looked to me to finish the sentence.

And then your solicitor finally chipped in with, 'He's been here ten days now and during that time he's settled down to the point where he feels he should be discharged.'

'How do you feel about the release?' asked the social worker of your psychiatrist.

I turned to this man who could have been anyone's grandfather. When I'd met with him to discuss your treatment, he'd told me you reminded him of his son. There but for the grace of your God, I'd thought at the time.

'Naturally, he's anxious to return home. That's something we're just as anxious for. However, in fairness, if we were to support his release we'd be doing him an injustice. You see, we're still juggling the medication and till we get that right, he needs to be here.'

Forgetting the supposed informality of it all, you again stood. This time the scraping of your chair sounded like a muffled scream. Fists clenched, you stood to attention and I was reminded of that night when you stood before your cub master earnestly promising to honour Queen and country. 'I'm okay now. I don't need medication. I'm going to join a fishing club...and a cricket club. Aren't I, Mum?'

I nodded, for that was exactly what you'd been talking about doing when you got out.

'And I don't need the medication. It's just that I, um, smoked too much marijuana. It made me feel things that weren't there.'

You stumbled, searching for what else you could say to prove your sanity. You looked down at me and never was I so proud, and yet so terrified.

The firing squad wasted no time in taking aim. 'And what does Mum think about her son being released?'

I stood beside you, held your hand. For the very first time since you'd been locked away, you truly looked into my eyes, beseeching me. I heard the dog's even breathing, the click of a biro, a ball hitting an outside wall. So softly I hoped no-one could hear, I said, 'I don't think he's ready to be released.'

I stared panic head-on. You'd heard. Stung, you clutched at fingers poking through gloves I'd bought to keep you warm. Still standing at attention, you watched, blinking too fast, as the jury conferred amongst themselves. Eventually the psychiatrist said: 'Based on your doctor's report, we've decided it's in your best interests you remain here. Of course, in a month we'll reassess your case. In the meantime, I'm sure when the time's right your doctor will give you overnight leave to help you assimilate back into the community.' They closed manila folders, and pocketed pens.

As chairs scuffed the wooden floor, you ran from the room, leaving the solicitor searching the air for a handshake. I followed you beneath dappled sunlight.

'It's because I love you...'

Jerky steps, stopping only when you reached the brick wall. Your shoulders twitched. Tentatively I rubbed your back like when you had colic all those years ago. Suddenly the weight of you was on me. You wrapped yourself around me, sobbing as hard as the time you were circumcised. Sobbing as hard as the time I did when you were ten days old and that long in the humidicrib.

'...that I have to do what's best for you.'

We sat on the wet grass, an arm around each other. 'Oh, Mum, this is so fucking hard. It's all so fucking hard. Everything's going so fast, it's gone before I know it.'

You rested your head on my shoulder, and I remembered a time, and so I told you. 'One Saturday when you were a kid, I was sick and so couldn't watch you play cricket. When you came home in your grass-stained whites, you looked upset. I asked what was wrong. "I stuffed up, Mum", you said. "Missed a catch that would've won us the match. It went so fast it was gone before I saw it". And I said something like, "Even when we've got our eyes open, we don't see what's coming at us".'

'What're you getting at?'

'I guess what I'm trying to say is, life eventually does fall into place, erratically or otherwise.'

'It's the otherwise that scares me.'

Though dampness seeped through my slacks, I didn't move, didn't want the moment to end. It was so long since you'd cried, since we held onto each other like we used to when we'd scare ourselves stupid watching a spooky movie. Afraid too, that if I broke the spell you'd call me a Judas Mother again.

We sat on the grass until the sun fell behind the brick wall.

'I have to go in for tea now. If I miss out I go hungry.'

'I'll be back tomorrow then.'

'Promise?'

'Promise.'

My bum was wet from the grass. As I walked to my car parked under a security light, all I could think on was, would you trust me to visit tomorrow?

Soft rain and sporadic windscreen wipers. I crest the hill near home. A rainbow, so huge, appeared. I stopped myself from turning the car in its direction, from chasing a rainbow that had no beginning or end to grab onto.

Dinner was bubbling away on the stove when I arrived home. I tried not to laugh at the sight of my husband wearing sunglasses as he cooked. To hide the bruises from the operation, I supposed.

'How is he?' asked my husband, as he plonked mashed potato on the plates.

'Every time I see him like this, it's as if parts of me are being ripped off.'

'It must be hard.' He concentrated on taking chops from the griller.

I called the boys who were in their rooms studying. Youngest son turned his nose up at the charred meat and lumpy potatoes. I gave him my 'don't you dare say a word' look.

It wasn't till we were halfway through the meal and no-one had mentioned you that I said, 'He lodged an appeal. It was heard today.'

'You didn't tell me!' said my husband.

'Is that like when you appeal to the umpire?' asked my youngest.

'What's he appealing against, Mum?' asked middle son.

'He doesn't want to stay in the hospital.'

'Why didn't you tell me?' repeated my husband.

'I guess, as his mother, I felt responsible.'

'As his stepfather, I share some of that responsibility too.'

He was right. I should've let him carry some of the load. But I hadn't even told my boss why I had to take an early lunch. I didn't want any witnesses to my betrayal. A necessary betrayal, but one nonetheless.

'Is he getting better?' asked my youngest.

'He might never get better, Darling. Might seem to, but keep sliding into the unreal space he's in now.' My husband gave me one of his 'that's too much information' looks. I ignored him. If my boys could pose a question, they deserved an honest answer. 'See, the difficulty is, because he's been smoking marijuana like it's about to go out of fashion, that in itself could be masking his condition.'

'What do you mean?'

'Well, it could be cannabis psychosis or schizophrenia.'

'What's…?'

Suddenly, it was me who wanted to escape the truth. I went outside and took deep, deep breaths. The day was nearly dead. With darkness the kittens seemed to get a new perspective, jumping in the air, mouths snapping at things only they could see, and I thought of you.

Chapter 9

You had a possible weekend leave and your voice trembled as you checked, yet again, that I'd be having the day off work Friday so that I could collect you from the 'prison', as you called it. You were like a tour director, not leaving anything to chance. 'Of course it all depends on my doctor,' you told me for the third day running. 'He'll give the thumbs-up on the Friday morning and then I'll ring you. It all depends on the doctor, though.'

On Friday the sun shone. I picked yellow and white daisies and put them in a vase on the table facing the door. I wanted them to be the first thing you saw. I dressed carefully, as if going on a date, discarding this pair of tailored pants for these jeans, then deciding on cords. Makeup couldn't hide the shadows under my eyes, nor the lines that had recently appeared at the corners of my mouth.

It was almost noon. I kept checking the phone for dial tone. Perhaps I should phone, or even just go there and wait? No, the nurse said they'd let me know if, and when, to pick you up. Anyway, I wanted to play it low-key, not smother you with my concern. I tried to settle by reading the day's headlines, then played around with the crossword, even read the comics, something I hadn't done since I was a kid and 'Dagwood' and 'Blondie' were all the rage.

When the doorbell rang, I was taking out a container of your sausage rolls from the freezer. Probably Mormons. I'd seen the young, suited men in the area over the last few days. I'd get rid of them quickly, tell them I was a Catholic.

Instead of dewy-eyed boys dressed up as men, I opened the door to you, my six-foot son whose eyes told more than most people could bear.

'Where did you come from?' I hugged you and looked to the street to see who had dropped you off.

'They told me I could take off.'

'How did you get here?'

'Jumped a train. Didn't have any money.'

Plonking your backpack on the table, you opened the fridge and stared into it like you always did, as if it held the answer to your hunger. I hugged you from behind, startled at how your ribs stuck out, distraught at how you trembled.

After drinking milk from the carton you headed for the hearth.

'I've been waiting for a phone call from you. Why didn't you…?'

You were totally focused on lighting the paper beneath the kindling.

'Why didn't you ring for me to collect you?'

'They said I could go. So I did.'

I made a mental note to call the nurse and demand to know why someone as sick as you could be left to fend for himself. As the microwave zapped the sausage rolls, I watched you poke at the reluctant fire. Away from that institution, from the mad others, I could really see you. How lanky you were. How the flickering flames accentuated the strain on your face. You reminded me of a hungry hunter who has returned to the cave, only the fire to keep you safe.

'I'm warming sausage rolls. Do you want some?'

'Wood, just wood. We need wood.'

On the way to the woodpile I passed the compost bin. I lifted the lid and smelt the decay that would eventually renew so much, and felt reassured. I loaded half a dozen gum logs into my arms and as I rounded the corner of the house I could see you through the glass door. Huddled over the fire, blowing at the struggling flames. I retraced my steps, dumped the gum logs, and filled the wheelbarrow to overflowing with the remains of the century old oak tree. Wood we kept for special occasions, wood that burnt under any conditions.

For a time we sat quietly, you stirring only to poke at the fire, me to gather an armful of wood from the wheelbarrow parked outside the door. Your face was flushed now, still I stacked the wood onto the fire, afraid you'd start trembling again.

'I'm never going back to that place. Never. Not ever.'

'Do you want some sausage rolls?'

'When in doubt, feed them!' you said, with your crooked smile. 'You always do that Mum. Like food is your ammunition.'

'Huh! More like armour.'

'After a while, you said, 'This is good,' arm sweeping the room.

'Yes. It is.'

'I'm not going back there, you know.'

'How's Dame Wilhelmina going? She still in there?'

'Still looking for her parrot.'

'And you. How are you feeling?'

'Pretty good. My shrink reckons I'll be discharged soon. But under a Community Order.'

'Sounds like Big Brother'll be watching you.' As usual, I spoke before I thought, but you laughed off my foot-in-mouth.

'It's their way of making sure I front up for the magic weekly injection.' As you said this, you held your hand over the flames.

'Not so close! You'll burn yourself!'

'I don't feel pain anymore. Look!'

Before I could reach out, you put you hand in the flames. I grabbed your arm, jerked it away. 'What in the hell do you think you're doing!'

'You worry too much.' Then, so proudly, you said, 'I'm protected now.'

'Protected from what?'

'From any things that might hurt me.'

'And what are they?' I sensed your silence was a way of protecting me from the horrors that assailed you. 'Please, don't put your hand in the fire. You don't have to prove anything to me.'

Like Siamese bookends, the cats sat at the glass door peering in. I envied them, their emotionally flat lives. 'They've got fat,' you said. 'You feed them too much. Fat slows you down, you know.'

Was that why you'd become so skinny? Because you had to be ahead of the game? I thought it was because of your metabolism; the fact that your mind was constantly speeding.

'I shouldn't be in there, you know.' Quick side-glance at me. Your way of telling me I did the wrong thing in not supporting the appeal.

'I have to do what I think is best for you.' My catch-cry that was wearing thin, even on me.

'Mothers don't know everything.'

'I only know what I see. And you're not well.'

I followed you outside to where you sat under the grapevine. Your fingers shook so, you had trouble rolling the paper around the tobacco.

'Have one of mine.' I offered you the pack I kept beside the barbeque.

'Nah. They're full of poison.'

This was one time I didn't have to be suspicious of your accusation.

Dragging deeply, you blew smoke rings and I watched as they disappeared. Suddenly you became agitated, your focus on a thistle growing amongst weeds. Kneeling, you pulled at the weeds, scattering them willy-nilly. 'That's a marijuana plant!' You indicated the thistle. 'Weeds are like poison. They sap the goodness. You should cultivate it better.'

'That's a thistle!'

'It's a marijuana plant.' You scoffed at my ignorance.

'Truly, it's a thistle.'

'Feed it. Weed it. And watch out for those helicopters.'

'Look at how much blossom's on the peach tree,' I said, trying to ground you in my reality.

Still kneeling, you stared at the far corner of the yard where a plum tree also grew. Stared for ages. Then, 'Why didn't I get one?'

'What…?'

'A fruit tree. My brothers both got one. Why didn't I?'

'But…but you were fifteen when we moved here. You'd never shown any interest in gardening. Your brothers were what? Three and five…I guess…I just thought…'cause you didn't live with us…'

'He got a peach tree, he got a plum tree. Where's mine?'

An invisible fist punched me in the stomach. I clutched your cold fingers. 'Come with me.'

'Where?'

'You'll see.'

I locked the house. Led you to the car. Me dressed for a date, you in the institutional uniform of a beanie and gloves with fingers poking through.

At the nursery you were like Goldilocks, but instead of chairs, trees. Rejecting this one for its branches were out of shape; that one for it was too short; then…this one 'because it just feels right'.

Once home you dug a hole, a perfect circle, aligning it with your brothers' fruit trees. After banging in a wooden stake, you anchored the apricot tree to it with one of my cast-off stockings. You stood back, checked from all angles, promised me we'd get lots of fruit. As long as I weeded and regularly fed it, not like the marijuana bush!

We sat in the sun on the brick terrace, saying nothing, with just the sound of rubbish trucks emptying our bins. You stood, stretched, and I marvelled at you, at how I had produced such a perfect body.

'What's for dinner, Mum?'

'Ammunition or armour. Take your pick.'

'Curried sausages?'

'If you like.'

'You can't imagine how much you think of food at that place. That's all you've got to look forward to. Pathetic really.'

'What do you think about, when you're not thinking about food?'

You stared at the sky. 'A kaleidoscope of images. Sometimes so many I feel colour-blind.'

'Good or bad ones?'

'Turbulent.' You stared at the sky, eyes screwed tight. 'Like snapshots in a whirlpool.'

When your brothers came home from school and were bombarding you with questions of 'How long are you going to stay?' 'Do you want a game of cricket?' Or, 'Let's play Nintendo!', you managed to toss in an aside of how you, too, now had a fruit tree. I watched from the kitchen window as the three of you stood admiring the apricot tree, heads nodding up at your animated face, hands gesticulating as you talked non-stop.

How could I have overlooked you, assumed you wouldn't be interested in having your 'very own tree'? I hadn't meant to exclude you from the family, your family. How much was I to blame for your illness? Your father? Stepfather? Could it be me and not a gene gone awry?

I sat in the lounge with a mug of chamomile. It was grey outside now, that time when the sun has fallen from the sky and the world seems to catch its breath. My thoughts wandered, spilling over with recriminations. Of the times when you went to live with your father in his three bedroom house, how he put you in a caravan out the back, as if you were a lodger and not his son. His de facto's children were used to having a bedroom to themselves. So, for nearly two years, you were exiled to the back yard. You didn't care, you told me. But you must have! Must have hated the isolation. On one of the rare occasions when I was forced to speak with your father, I did say how wrong the set-up was, that being relegated to live in the backyard was like keeping a pup out of the kennel. I should have asserted myself more but, though it was twelve years since that violent night, I still hadn't regained my strength or courage. Twelve years that felt like twelve hours. Did you remember that night? I prayed you didn't.

I recalled another memory of you always struggling with school-work. Nowadays you would have been labelled with Attention Deficit Disorder. It was Year 9 at school report time. Your step-father's affection was often overridden by a strict sense of respon-sibility. He was the one who spent time taking you through difficult homework, helping with projects. But then, he was also your mate, spending hours playing cricket, teaching you how to hold a bat, to spin bowl; fishing with you on the banks of the Warrandyte River, or off St Kilda Pier, kicking a football in the park, and cheering on your footy team with you. Once when your stepfather was working interstate, and there was a Father & Son Sex Education night at school, there was no choice but for me to attend with you. The only woman in an auditorium of men and boys! In all your school years, your father never attended a function, not even when you graduated from primary school. It was your stepfather who kept in regular contact with your school coordinators and teachers, wanting you to do well, feeling frus-trated when nothing seemed to work to your advantage, or when you just didn't seem to care.

'You'd better bring home a good school report,' your step-father said to you one night after tea, 'Or else I'll thrash the living daylights out of you.'

I was changing your brothers' nappies and remember thinking, well you know he's not going to get a good school report 'cause you've been in touch with the teachers and they've told you just that. Was he expecting a miracle over the last month? The thing about the thrashing was just all bluff, I knew that. I thought you would've too.

The next night you came home from school and immediately began to work on your bike, pulling it to bits. You often did this, dismantling things to see how they ticked over, or made a sound. But you had trouble putting them back together. After tea, and well into the night, your stepfather helped you piece it back together, made it roadworthy again.

'Here's my report,' you said, throwing it on the table the next afternoon when you returned from school.

A baby on the hip, the other in the highchair, I called out to your retreating back, 'I'll read it in a tic. Once I get the kids settled.'

Within minutes you reappeared with an overnight bag, which you'd obviously packed the night before. 'I'm off.' You kissed me on the cheek. I followed you to the garage.

'Off where?'

'I'm going to Nan's. The report's no good.'

'You can't. It doesn't matter about the report. You can't leave me.'

I was still mouthing 'you can't leave me' as you furiously pedalled up the street.

Now my mug was empty and the greyness had almost turned to black. Still the three of you stood around the apricot tree nattering away to each other. I can still feel the physical pain of that time when you pedalled away from me. You never really returned to us despite a few aborted attempts. There were always regular weekend visits, but you never wanted to be fully part of us again.

Distance should make things fuzzier, so why does revisiting the past give such clarity? I can feel the bottled anger I felt at my husband for making such a threat, an idle threat, but one just the same. I tried to understand why he was often so rigid. He never talked much about his childhood but one story sticks in my mind…of how each night my husband, as a boy, had to sweep a large square of the road so his father could park his car on a clean spot.

'Anyone'd think it was the middle of winter,' said my husband, shedding his jacket and tie when he came home from work. He kissed me on the cheek.

'The fire helps settle him down.'

'How is he?'

'Hard to say.'

I could see the worry cloud on his face as he went to say hello.

Like an ordinary family, we sat at the dinner table, the cats put out at you sitting in what they considered their spot. Nearly every mealtime, like figurines with moveable eyes, they sat on your chair hoping for a handout.

Whenever the five of us came together there was, for the shortest time, a 'settling-in' space that allowed for the shift in dynamics. That space was even more pronounced this evening.

'I bought you home some shredded paper for the compost,' said my husband.

'Great. I'm just about ready to start on another bin. What's there is ready to be dug in.'

'Jupiter's the vacuum cleaner of our galaxy,' you said.

'Really? How so?' said my husband, warily, as I tried to fathom how that statement fitted in with the conversation.

'I was reading, its gravitational pull is so strong it draws comets and other space debris into its atmosphere.'

For a minute there I thought you were losing it.

'Then why hasn't Haley's Comet been sucked up?' said your brother.

'It just sucks up things that're out of orbit.' You laughed, then added, 'Just wayward stuff. It just sucks up wayward stuff, otherwise we wouldn't be here.'

'You'd better be careful then!' said your brother, giggling.

You flicked a pea at him, and, suddenly, the space wasn't there anymore. This is what I loved most about you guys; the way you gave each other so much slack, the way you treated each other the same, whether sick or well.

'I got my 'Learners', you know,' you said.

'In there?' said my husband, meaning the hospital.

'Oh yeah, sure. Most of us can't remember what day it is, let alone sit for a test.'

'Before then,' I said.

'How many questions did you get wrong?' said my husband.

'Three. Four and you're out. It's all done on computer, by multiple choice.'

'So where's this leading to?'

You turned an imaginary wheel, pushed the palm of your hand in the air and made a tooting sound. Your brothers cracked up, as they often did at your whacky sense of humour. This is funny, I thought, so why aren't I laughing?

'What I mean is,' continued my husband, 'I hope you don't think you can run a car while you're on the dole!'

'You can borrow my car. I don't need it every day,' I said.

'That's not the point!' My husband pushed himself away from the table.

'So what is the point?' I said.

'It's okay, Mum. Leave it,' you said.

'What is the bloody point!' I said.

'Look, I don't come home from a hard day's work to be bothered with all this,' said my husband looking as if he'd been assaulted.

'I'm going for a walk,' you said, leaving us hanging with our anger.

When you'd left, the boys went to their rooms. Before long the usual accompaniment to homework blared through the house. While Pearl Jam sang about life, I couldn't put a seal on my rage.

'Why must you do this! Why? Answer me. Why?'

'I'm just teaching him values,' said my husband. 'He has to learn that nothing comes free.'

My knuckles were white from gripping the edge of the table. 'I want to hit you! I want to slap your face backwards and forwards until you see what you do!'

'What I do!'

'After all he's been through, he knows that everything has a price.'

'He bought it on himself. If he hadn't been sucking on marijuana all these years he wouldn't be in hospital.'

'So what if he did! What if he fucking did!'

'Tone your language.'

'What does it matter in the scheme of things? The fact remains he's been in hell. And that alone deserves a bit of compassion. You could at least have congratulated him. He was so excited…wanted to tell you himself. Managing to get through that test was a big effort.'

'Yes it was. It's just that…'

I left him then and went to the bedroom and sat on the edge of the bed until I heard you come back from wherever you'd been walking.

In the morning a steel-sharp scratching sound woke me, along with a thumping headache. 'Must you do that?' I murmured. For years I'd been asking my husband to quietly select a shirt.

'Well buy plastic coat hangers then!'

I stared at the crack in the ceiling, thought that I should get up and see the boys off to school. You'd be asleep, you always slept late. I felt heavy and didn't move until I heard the front door slam. My husband was reversing down the driveway when he saw me. 'I need extra money,' I said, finding it difficult to swallow.

'What's happening with us?' he said.

'I just feel so sad.'

'Yeah, I know you how feel,' he said, opening his wallet. 'Lately, I'm exhausted too.' I studied his face. It was shut, truculent. 'So how much do you want?'

'Fifty'll do. I thought we'd see a movie or something.' He flipped the wallet open and held it out to me. I had to loosen the notes myself.

When my husband had gone off to immerse himself in work, and the boys had gone to school, I sat nursing a cold coffee, staring at the shimmering reflections on the pool. He mustn't have heard me properly, comparing my sadness to his tiredness. But then, perhaps he did. Perhaps it was my sadness that was exhausting him. I shivered at the feeling that so often flooded me now. Like I was missing something important like an arm or leg.

Chapter 10

The place I'm looking for is behind a Drop-In Centre. I'm early and don't want to make a conspicuous entrance, so sit awhile in the car, the seven o'clock news as company. Drop-In Centre. Is there a door to this Centre or does one gain access by falling through the roof?

The sombre voice detailing the news tells me nothing out of the ordinary. Here in this city random murders take place, and the elderly are duped out of life savings. War continues to rage in the Middle East, while an eight-year-old boy caught in the firing line is shot dead. And I feel nothing. It's hard to feel when an inner war rages unabated, depleting my emotional ammunition, random bullets leaving me pot-holed, ricochets of hissing grief that make me gasp for air.

I lock the car and go into this supposed place of refuge.

In the cold hall a semi-circle of plastic chairs fills a corner. A dusty piano is relegated to the farthest corner. On the whiteboard, fixed to the wall, are details of the groups that use this hall. One for nearly every day of the week, it seems – anonymous ones of Alcoholics, Overeaters, Gamblers, then Grief Support, and, stuck on the end as the name implies, a Decoupage Group.

One by one they wander in, these people who need support. One man studies the racing guide, a woman begins to crochet, others stare at the fifty-year-old portrait of the Queen that hangs crookedly beside the whiteboard. I study these people with the same number of arms and legs, identical people hollowed from sorrow.

The young woman who sits beside me offers her hand. I introduce myself, and wonder what type of grief she has faced. Type of grief? Is there a grief ladder delineating the range – low, medium, high, for parent, partner, child? So caught up in the grief ladder, I nearly miss my introduction. The facilitator in sandshoes invites me to say a few words.

'My son hung himself,' I say. No looks of horror, of pity. Just steady, knowing eyes waiting for me to continue. I provide the barest of details, then add, 'I guess I'm here looking for a soft landing.' I sit down in the palpable silence.

Someone eventually says, 'You must be angry with him.' I look, but whoever asked the question won't meet my eyes.

I want to slap people who ask if I'm angry with you for what you did. 'It's one of the stages' say these people who obviously have a degree in grief. The only stage I feel is guilt. Like when I find myself, head thrown back as if to catch the breeze from my laughter. Or when I look in the mirror and like what I see. If I go four hours without thinking on you. For not having taken enough photos. Even guiltier that I only gave you twenty dollars that time. And for silly things like plucking my eyebrows (as if they matter in the scheme of things).

The next person to take centre stage is the old man who wears braces and a peaked cap. He stands, supported by his walker. 'Today is the anniversary of when my Myrtle left me.' He wipes at his eyes with the back of his hand. 'I kissed her good night, but she wasn't there to kiss good morning.'

'Every week we go through the same old thing,' says the massive woman beside me, who could have been at the wrong group.

'When did she die?' I whisper.

'She didn't. Walked out on him twenty years ago.'

A woman in a hot pink pantsuit raises her hand. 'I finally did it,' she says. 'Five years it's taken me, but yesterday I went to her grave.'

'And how did you feel?' asks the facilitator.

'Freed up. I felt freed up. Five years it's taken me.'

The others clap, and she smiles as though she's just graduated.

The group falls silent. I look to the facilitator, but she waits till someone's ready to expose more of themselves. Then:

'I don't know how much longer I can go on like this. I never imagined pain could weigh so much,' says the massive woman, turkey neck wobbling.

This is not what I expected. There's no emotional touching, everyone separate in their grief. It's not contagious, I want to shout. Anyway, you've already got it, so don't be afraid to touch. Instead, I look at the whiteboard, wishing it was Wednesday night, for then I'd be anonymously at Overeaters, filled to the brim with superfluous food instead of dissolving from grief.

There's a long silence. I want to say something, for my silence only makes me untouchable, and so I tell them, 'When I lost my son, I lost my memory. The shopping list had to be written and not imagined. At work, I couldn't recall which of the four keys unlocked the safe, couldn't recall the names of my colleagues and so everyone became 'love', or 'sweetie'.

Their nods encourage me to continue.

'Chunks of me fell off when my son died. My memory shrivelled from the shock. I still have to think twice what my address is. And yet, I have no trouble remembering my son's address. Houghton Lawn, Grave No. 3867.'

The man in the peaked cap says: 'I wish I had a grave to visit. A grave would be comforting, sort of.'

'Closure,' says the woman in hot pink. 'It gives you closure.'

Can there ever be closure? A settling down of the ache, but closure?

I'd been thinking of revisiting your grave over the last few weeks, but kept rejecting the idea for I'd only find it depressing and anyway, you're with me every day. When I did go, it was ostensibly to check the plaque had been engraved as I'd wanted.

My shadow covered the rectangle that was a clay mound last time I was here, and was now carpeted with lawn. Keeping you warm. In my head I talked to you. Told you, some say I must feel angry at you. How can I? When every time I breathe it hurts. A wide hole that lets in the moaning wind to rattle my senses. If you hurt like this every time you took a breath, then how can I be angry that you decided to stop breathing?

I told you, some say I have so much to rejoice over. What they mean is, they don't know how to make it better. But, in a sense, they are right for when I think on you I rejoice that I knew you, that you knew me.

I told you some people say in their conversations with me, 'When he was first dead'. Do they think that there are parts to death like seasons? First dead: a frozen Wintery state; recently dead: the shocked stillness of Autumn; died some time ago: Spring growth emerging from the bone compost; a long time dead: sultry Summer, sweating tears.

In that damp place a bumblebee spun its wings as a toy windmill went berserk. In that place my heart heaved, desperate to join you. I didn't cry in that place. But coming to and going from, tears filled the sockets of my sorrow. In that place where flowers drooped at headrests, I sat on your grass blanket. No flowers. Just unspoken words that clenched my gut, jammed my heart. The least I could have done was to give you my tears to keep the grass green.

On the sunken grave, just four holes away, there was a stray flower. A gerbera. I scattered its petals over you. Crimson on green.

Gums murmured in the breeze, the smoke from my cigarette blew towards the waterfall that seemed to spring from nowhere. I stubbed out the cigarette and started for home to watch *The Bold and the Beautiful*. Just as I crested the hill to the car park, yet another procession began. In the cover of a gum I watched. Practicalities came first, the opening of the boot, a collapsible chair for the one who grieves the most. I wanted it to be a coffin, white like the minister's robes, needed to know I wasn't alone, needed another mother, a stranger to mutely comfort me.

'I'm sick to death of hearing that word.' The loud voice centres me in the present. It's the massive woman. 'Closure! There's no such thing. Shit, if there was closure, we all wouldn't be here, would we? Bloody trendy word that means nothing!'

'What frightens me the most,' says the woman in the hot pink outfit, 'is I'm afraid my daughter will follow her sister.'

She's talking about copy-catting. I haven't told your brothers what happened the night after your funeral, afraid they might get on the same roundabout. At the wake, your best mate and I spent time talking, me trying to allay the guilt he felt at not seeing how deep your despair went. Just two nights before you died, he took you fishing with a few other blokes you'd known for years. While they sat dangling their legs on St. Kilda Pier, you paced the boardwalk.

'Come on mate, throw a line in,' he'd said.

You did, but only for a moment. Pacing again. One minute he heard your footsteps, the next you were gone. You left your wallet beneath the plastic bag of bait. They waited for you, your mates, waited for hours, waited until the slab of beer ran out.

'Turned out he caught the first train home,' your mate said. 'Dunno what he did during the time he left us till then.'

I knew. You told me. But I didn't say, for it would add to his despair.

When the wake was nearly over, the mourners slowly dispersing like their footy team had lost, I came across your brothers having a game of billiards with your best mate. Heard him say, 'He really loved you two, you know. Was always talking about the weekends he spent with you. He was so proud of everything you did. Drove me mad half the time, the way he'd go on about you two.' Your brothers said nothing. They already knew.

The next night your best mate, and the same blokes who'd gone fishing off St. Kilda Pier, were continuing the wake at the local pub. Your mate asked his brother for five dollars, said he was hungry, wanted to buy some Kentucky Fried Chicken. He didn't go to the chicken shop. Instead, he went to the hardware shop.

His brother found him a few hours later, hanging from a tree in the local park. The price tag still on the rope – 'Special - $4.95'. A note in his pocket. 'I want to be with my best mate. Bury me with him.'

I wrote to his mother, whom I'd never met, said I would be honoured if she buried her son alongside mine. That my son's gravesite had room for two coffins. She buried her son on the other side of town, far away from you.

'I think it's time we had a cuppa,' says the facilitator, as I blink my way into the present.

I watch them mill around the urn, deliberating over the biscuits on the paper plate. I'm wondering whether I should be here, if this group can give me what I want, need, when the massive woman settles beside me.

'What do you think about Limbo?' she says.

The Limbo Rock comes to mind, but then I understand.

'My daughter's in Limbo.'

'Oh?'

'I went to this fortune teller. She said that's why I can't get in touch with her.' She crams a cream biscuit into her mouth. 'Do you think it's a beautiful place?' She spits crumbs at me.

'I'm sure it is.' How can I tell her it's a dislocated island, unreachable by warmth. Limbo is where pieces of me are scattered. Cowpats, solidified by guilt.

'She reckoned you stay there until you're forgiven.'

'By whom?'

She looks at me as if I have the answer.

'Forgiven by God, us earthlings, or even themselves?' I say.

She shakes her head and her chin disappears in the folds of flesh. She leaves me to go replenish her biscuits.

Are you in Limbo, too, or have you been promoted? I imagine your Limbo to be a place of isolation where others can't reach. Are you there until forgiveness settles like dandruff, unable to be shrugged off?

Hang on, what if you are stuck in Limbo until I forgive myself?

'We need to move on. We do have time constraints,' says the facilitator, adding, 'The decoupage ladies will be here at eight-thirty.'

I imagine women, bent over, scissoring away at pretty images they'll stick on something ugly, then lacquering the images so nothing will mar the artificial beauty. I try to imagine what they would think of us, these scissoring ladies. When we leave the hall, is the air filled with an invisible stain that permeates their joy?

'…and I should have known,' says the young woman beside me. 'When he gave away his childhood toys, I should have known. He said he was just sick of the clutter.'

I'm still in two minds about whether to return to the group, but my decision is made when the facilitator concludes with, 'It helps us to remember that no living person is a stranger to loss. The rebirth of the soul is both an agony and a joy. You are all in an agonising state. Joy will follow, believe me. And never forget how precious life is.'

How fucking dare she! I don't need to be told that life is precious, for too often I'm reminded when the black prod of death sears, buckling me from the heat.

Driving home, I berate myself for thinking I'd find comfort from others who were in the same hellhole. I'd been expecting a daisy-chain of support, not people so weighted in their misery that they couldn't bear the brunt of another's. All that I got out of the group was that these people had survived, proof that I, too, might.

I park the car in the street, and sit there awhile, staring at the flickering streetlight. Physical torture would be easier to bear than this relentless ache. I should have kicked your teeth in, ripped your eyes out, burnt matches under your nails, then given you a Chinese burn. No, not to punish you, but to make you feel enough to stay.

'How'd it go?' asks my husband, even before I've closed the front door. He sits at the kitchen table, television off, newspaper before him. The house is too quiet.

'Yeah, good. Where are the boys?'

'Gone to the movies.'

'Right.'

'Do you want a cuppa?'

'I think I'll go to bed.' Alone, I want to say.

'Yeah, I'll get an early night, too.'

In bed, I pretend to read.

'What did you do today?' My husband lies beside me, his hand resting on my thigh. I shrug it off, tell him it's too heavy. He sighs.

'What did the boys go to see?'

'Some comedy.'

'So what did you do today?' he again asks.

'Nothing out of the ordinary. Just work, rushed home and threw a meal together, then went to the support group.'

No, nothing out of the ordinary. Worked, cooked, searched, as behind the mask I slipped and dipped to that place where reality waits as sure as my unmarked tombstone, waits, demanding surrender to the simple pain of losing you.

I close the book, turn the lamp off, and snuggle far down into the doona. My husband fits his body to mine. I wrap my cold feet around his legs.

'I miss him so,' I say, surprised at speaking my thoughts.

'I know you do.'

'Why don't you ever say his name, or remember things aloud?'

He says nothing. Just sighs, and puts his hand on my thigh.

No-one speaks your name now. Not unless I nudge them into reminiscing. I rail at the thought you might be forgotten, castigate those who look away at the mention of your name. And yet…this week I forgot your birthday, remembered a day later. I don't know whether my swamping grief stems from guilt, or the mere fact you would have been thirty-one.

'I think of him,' says my husband, and I sense he is crying inside. Then, after a while, 'Will you go to the group again?'

'Yes.' I have no intention of going back. Next week, on the same night, I shall go to a café, drink coffee, and return home at the appropriate time. My husband found the group for me. I don't want to disappoint him.

'I'm so glad,' he says. 'You can't do this on your own. You need support.'

He thinks that someone will be there to catch me when I fall.

Whatever, there is no soft landing.

Chapter 11

I'm naked, trembling in the steam-filled room, the shower still running. I'd been about to hop in when the phone rang, your psychiatrist returning my call. That word he mentioned, as if just a by-line. I know what it is, what it means. Each week now the media promotes a particular subject to highlight an illness or need. Recently there's been Motor Neurone, the Homeless, Freedom from Hunger, Keep Australia Beautiful; the list goes on. And coincidentally, two weeks ago, schizophrenia. Though your diagnosis was incomplete, I saturated myself in the media information. The high suicide rate of those suffering the terror that is schizophrenia is mind boggling, as is the ignorance of people as to what that disease is.

Why, just the other day, I was pushing a trolley around the supermarket, when I got a tap on the shoulder.

'How are you?' Mrs Know-It-All ex-neighbour.

'Fine, I'm fine thanks.'

She lowered her voice. 'I'm so sorry to hear the news. How's he going?'

'He's coming along.'

'It must be sooo difficult. You must sometimes wonder whether you're Arthur or Martha.'

'What do you mean?'

She lowered her voice even more, and I had to strain to hear. 'Well, trying to cope with a son who has schizophrenia must keep you on your toes.' She leant closer. 'I saw 'The Three Faces of Eve'. You must wonder which personality's going to pop up from day to day.'

I parked my trolley beside the toilet rolls. Gripped her trolley tight. 'Yes, my son has schizophrenia,' I said, so loud she backed off. 'It's a mental illness that has nothing to do with multiple personalities. It's when one is out of touch with reality. Something that obviously affects a lot of us.'

She arched an eyebrow. Whether because my barb had hit home, or because my booming voice was making a spectacle of us, I didn't care. 'Well,' she said, 'you're in my prayers, anyway.'

'Thank you,' I said, adding, 'Just make sure you're praying to the right saint.'

Where had Miss Pleasant gone, the me who was always trying to appease? By the time I got to the meat section, I'd decided Miss Pleasant had disappeared somewhere between Judas Mother and the appeal.

The idea of showering no longer appeals to me, and I turn off the water, wrap myself in the chenille dressing gown and do what my mother did in times of stress. Put the kettle on. I'm surprised at how forthcoming your shrink was, sharing with me what you'd disclosed to him. But it's probably different with mental illness. The boundaries of confidentiality are necessarily blurred as family members need to be informed because they're usually the ones who end up as the carers.

I still wanted to believe your bizarre behaviour was caused by overdosing on marijuana. Your psychiatrist said that it might be the cause, but it was the result we needed to look at. Cannabis psychosis…psychotic cannibals. Whichever, the tag that was sticking was schizophrenia.

As I clear the breakfast table, I wonder what you are doing now in the flat you share with your best mate. You're probably still under the doona. Five days you stayed with us after discharge from the hospital. You'd been pretty even, not freaking out or imagining things, and because I couldn't find any marijuana stashed in your room, I put your evenness down to not getting into any. If you'd only stayed with us a few more weeks, I could've kept you on track.

'I can count out two white tablets and two purple tablets, Mum,' you'd insisted when I asked you to stay just a bit longer. It wasn't the tablets I was worried about. Back in your old hunting ground would be your supplier.

It's only a week since you left us and in that time, there's been moments when I found your absence a tranquil relief. But there's been hours of hand-wringing, and trying to swallow the foreboding I feel. I scrunch the empty egg shells. They're near translucent, yet still won't compost unless first pulverised. I put my uneaten eggs in the fridge for lunch and recall the tension at breakfast.

'Is that all you're having? Just coffee?' said my husband.

'I can't eat.'

'You'll make yourself sick. And then you'll be no good to any of us.'

'What if he's got schizophrenia?'

'Rubbish! It's that shit he smokes, and as far as I'm concerned there's no sympathy when it's self-inflicted.'

'How can you sit there so smugly...'

'Jesus, as if I haven't got enough on my plate!' He shook the newspaper. 'Let him go for Christsakes!' His face was hidden behind the paper, leaving me to stare at the back page where above the headline, 'Let the Games Begin', was a photo of three Australian swimmers – Olympians, who stood straight and tall, their eyes showing a single-mindedness. I hated them, these strangers with their ability to be so focused.

I laughed as my husband neatly lopped the top of his egg.

'What's so funny?'

'Even Humpty Dumpty had it bad,' I said. 'There he was minding his own bloody business, and whack! he couldn't be put back together again.'

'I don't understand?'

'Neither do I.' I wasn't laughing now. 'Neither do I.'

He put his hand on mine. Held it still. I hadn't noticed my nervous tremor. 'Look, I know you're worried, Sweetie. But he'll be fine.'

'You can't know that.'

'Well, none of us will know the rate you're going.'

'What's that supposed to mean?' He left the table. I stood in front of him. 'Don't' start that caper with me!'

'What caper?'

Leave me hanging without an explanation…as if I'm just a blank in those bloody cryptic crosswords of yours.'

He sighed. 'What I meant was, and don't take this the wrong way, is it's time you cut the cord. It's stretched as far as it'll go.'

After he went to work, I sat at the kitchen bench watching the hands on the clock as they dropped through time. Was I the sort of mother who couldn't, wouldn't let go?

I'm still caught up in this dilemma as I wander out to the compost bin, my usual first port of call, even if there are no kitchen scraps to tip. I toss in the egg shells and peer at how the worms work the mass of rubbish. Sometimes I stand for ages, a hand on top of the mound, feeling the warmth emanating from what was once considered worthless.

The doorbell rings. I should disconnect it. A bell one must hear, a knock one can pretend not to hear.

It's FF. I met her when I was pregnant with you. A Forever Friend, yours and mine. She glides in smelling, as usual, of turpentine.

'How are you?' she asks.

I smile at how she looks like a speckled egg. 'You've been at the easel already?'

'I treat each day as though it could be my last. Time waits for no-one!' she says in a ponderous voice. Then, gently, 'How are you?'

'Oh, I've got the can't-be-bothereds.'

'And what's brought that on?'

'Oh, this and that.'

'This being your pride and joy. That being the fear of the unknown?'

'You know me too well.'

'How is he?' She flicks the button on the kettle, then sets out mugs.

'If I said, fine, would you think he was normal? If I said bad, would you think he was mad?'

'You could have been a lyricist. Failing that, made a fortune from singing telegrams!'

'Actually, he's been pretty good. Just the occasional loop-out which, if I didn't have my antennae up, I probably wouldn't've noticed.'

'We're all loopy. Some of us are just better at hiding it.'

I watch as she dunks teabags in the water. Then I ask her if she thinks I'm overprotective of you.

'You love him too much. But then, I'm not a mother so who am I to talk?'

'I'd hate to think I was the cause of all this. You know, one of those cloying mothers who suffocate her kid.'

'You're the one who encouraged him to get a flat. The one who scoured Op Shops, and auctions, to furnish it. You pushed him out of Grandma's nest. And so you should have. It was high time.' She lit a cigarette, offered me one. 'Come on, let's do something. A waste of time moping around on your day off.'

'No. I've got a stack of groceries I want to take over to him.'

'Well, unless you're going in your PJs, I'd suggest you get dressed, then we'll do just that.'

I didn't want her to go with me, but didn't know how to say no. All I'd told her was that you were out of touch with reality. How does someone who hasn't been face-to-face with a disjointed, hallucinatory mind interpret that scenario? That you get the days mixed up? All that happens on the 'X Files' is real?

I threw on a tracksuit, did my sneakers up in a double knot. 'If you don't do a double knot, you'll fall out of your shoes.' My mother's words. Here I was, the ripe old age of forty and, though common sense dictates you can't fall out of your shoes, I still did as Mum said. Habit? Or an illusionary fear that Mum's reality was right. I go to the bathroom, wash my hands and face, and say to the woman in the mirror, 'I guess reality boils down to the way each of us perceives it, don't you think?' And the woman in the mirror lowers her head onto the basin and sighs. Not a sigh of youth when you yearn for the future to hurry up, but deep exhalations like life itself's being sucked out of you.

'Hubby's not supporting you much through this, is he?' says FF as she expertly manoeuvres her jazzy car through mid-morning traffic.

'He has his good points.'

'Sure. So does a compass!'

'Please, leave it!'

Though we hadn't told you we were coming, you opened the door before we even knocked.

'Close the door, quick!' you said, staying hidden behind it.

I kiss you on the cheek. Your eyes stay on the driveway. I go to the fridge, store the food I've brought. Frozen pizzas, pies and Chiko rolls. Not much nutrition, but at least you'll eat because of the little effort it takes to prepare.

'You oughta tart this place up a bit. Put a few posters up,' says FF. 'I can do you a painting. An abstract, or…'

'Nah. Might not be staying long.' You peer through the venetians.

'Did you watch the opening of the Olympics?' I ask.

'Nah. Don't want anything to do with drugs.' Still you stare down the driveway.

'You expecting someone?' asks FF.

'They've got a contract on me.'

'Why?' she says, trying not to look disconcerted.

'I know everything, that's why. I'm the chosen one.' Hands fidget in your pockets as if looking for something to hang onto.

'Who chose you?' says FF.

You look to both of us. 'What's the message in the bible, FF?' Screaming now, 'What's the message in the Bible, Mum?'

'To live and let live,' I say, for want of something to say.

'You haven't read it, Mum, have you?' You sneer at me, then return to your vigil.

'Dribs and drabs,' I say, my stomach doing a flip at the possibility of what's to come.

'You have to get the message!'

'What is the message?' asks FF, so gently.

'I can't tell you.' Agitated now. 'Everyone has to find out for themselves.'

'So...how did you find out,' says FF. 'Did you read it somewhere?'

'No, I was told. I'm the chosen one.'

I peer into the freezer, note it needs defrosting, but decide that now's not the right time to start chipping at the ice with a knife. FF leads you from your lookout and sits you beside her on the couch, not saying anything, just rubbing your arm up and down and round and round, as though your circulation needs jump-starting. At first you study FF as though she holds the answer to something, or everything, and then you wrap your arms around her. And I am so envious. I kneel at your feet, fold my arms around your knees, tell you, 'I know you think that what's going down is real. But, believe me, it's not. What's going on in your head is real to you, but it's not to me.' You nod, but I can tell you're just agreeing to shut me up.

We eat rolls filled with ham and cheese. Thinly filled, as I want to leave as much food as I can. You hardly touch yours. You're up and down like a yo-yo, peering out the window.

'Have you taken your tablets today?' I ask.

'Don't you worry about me, Mum.'

How can I not? How can I not worry about you, my gentle giant who has a head full of buzzards screaming different things, demanding to be heard?

'Have you been smoking dope?' asks FF.

'Haven't touched the stuff for months. Smoked a lot before that, though. Grew these two humungous bushes, high as the fence they were. Had a ball.'

As I tidy up the flat, FF tries to cajole you into going for a walk, tells you that you need to get some sun on your handsome face, that you're looking peaky. You ponder the invitation, finally saying, 'Yes, my heartbeat's way too high. A walk will even it. Have to get it down.'

While you're both out, I spin from stripping sheets to mopping floors to wiping benches, anything to fill the tangled space in my mind. Then I sit on the porch steps, absentmindedly pulling at weeds that crowd the straggly fuchsia. I see you both coming, heads bowed in conversation.

'I've been trying to talk him into coming home with you for a few days. He needs fattening up.' Playfully she digs you in the ribs. 'He's starting to look like a refugee.'

How right you are, I think. 'What a good idea!' I say.

'Nah. Gotta stay where it's safe.' You hurry inside.

FF sits on the steps, puts an arm around me, whispers, 'He shouldn't be on his own.'

'But what do I do? Tie him up and drag him home?'

When it's time to make tracks, you seem reluctant for us to go, stalling by bringing things from beneath the couch. An old chess board that's held together with sticky tape, photo album, a dictionary with someone else's name on it. And a gold cross, set with a red stone. 'Very precious,' you tell us, then in the next breath say you got it for twenty dollars at the market, that chosen ones must have a cross.

To bear? I wonder, as I hug you. 'Come on, come home. Spend a few days with me.'

'I've got things to do.'

'What things?'

'Just things.' You look confused.

As FF reverses the car down the long driveway, you come running after us, arms flapping like a bird unable to take off. 'Can I come with you?'

'Of course, Darling, of course.'

While we wait for you to gather a few things, I ask FF what you were both talking about earlier on your walk.

'Lots of stuff. Some a bit whacky.'

'Like?'

'That he doesn't want to die. He wants a girlfriend, someone he can trust. That he remembers the time I took him to the zoo when he was a kid and he tried to scare me by pretending to jump into the bear's enclosure. And the rest you've heard…the stuff about the contract being out on him, being the chosen one. Oh yeah, and that he's had an angelic experience.'

As you lope down the driveway, a backpack clutched to your chest, FF says, 'What must it be like?'

'I can't imagine. Though I try to.'

So softly, I have to strain to hear, she says, 'He reminds me of a bag of licorice allsorts. All being nibbled at the same time.'

Chapter 12

The constant sliding of the glass door made me aware you were in and out, probably having a cigarette in the back yard. Then there was silence, too long a silence.

'Having trouble sleeping?' I asked, as I wrapped myself in the dressing gown. You were lying on the floor, the television muted.

'Those magic pills don't work as good as in hospital. And there's nothing much on, either.' You pointed the remote at the television, zapping it.

I made a cuppa for myself, a toasted sandwich for you. Cheese and gherkin, your favourite. Wanting a cigarette, we sat outside in the dark.

'It's too quiet around here,' you said, licking a finger to get up the last of the crumbs.

'It is three in the morning!'

'Even the cicadas have been silenced. I miss them. It's not summer without them.'

'Yeah, you're right,' I said, just then realising their musical backdrop to balmy nights had been missing.

'They reckon something's happened at the hatching stage this year. An unknown mass killer, or something.'

I didn't ask where you got this fact from. You were always a font of information, often trivial, but informative just the same. You never read books, instead pored over the newspaper, devouring everything – articles, advertisements, births and deaths even. Just yesterday I'd got you to come along to the library with me in the hope you'd borrow something. When we were leaving I asked why you didn't check anything out. Dyslexic, you told me. Always been dyslexic, just wasn't picked up at school. Always had trouble concentrating.

'Everything's so out of whack. Crazy,' you said, as we sat outside smoking beneath a moon that hung crooked.

I held my breath, waiting for yet another revelation of your turmoil.

'Even the cuckoo called five days early this year. It's the seasons. They're getting later and later.'

My laughter startled us both. You looked to me for an explanation, but I was laughing too much to give you one.

'That's the Milky Way,' you said, pointing to what I already knew. 'And that's the Southern Cross. Don't think they'll ever change. Always be our compass.'

'The only certainty in life,' I said, sober now, 'is nothing remains static.'

'If only...' you said, and I waited but you didn't finish your thought.

For a while, we sat in the dark silence, watching smoke from our cigarettes drift to nowhere. I suggested we go to bed, but you couldn't sleep, you said, too much going on. I didn't have to ask twice if you wanted to go inside for a game of cards.

I was concentrating on how many tricks I could win without the right bower, when you said, 'See how powerful I am.' I thought you were referring to the great hand I'd dealt you. 'See how powerful I am!' The urgency in your voice made me look up. Cupped in your hand was a burning Ace of Spaces. I reached for your hand. You stood, too tall for me to reach.

'Please, don't do this!'

'It doesn't hurt.' You watched the card burn to ash. 'See, I am all-powerful. Nothing can harm me.' You sat down and picked up your cards as though you'd just returned from getting a drink.

'Let me dress it.'

'All-powerful people don't get infections, Mum.' You smiled at me as though I had a lot to learn.

I didn't win a round after that, could hardly hold the cards, let alone see them, could only see the ash on the table.

Then later, it was I who couldn't sleep, who walked through the house like a prowler. You slept as though nothing untoward had happened, burnt hand resting palm up on the pillow. I cursed the system that had discharged you just two weeks ago with only a plastic bag of tablets and not even a referral to a psychiatrist.

I was still awake when Mr Next Door did his morning ritual of coughing up phlegm then flushing the toilet, was still lying in bed when your brother went into your room before going to school. Heard him ask if you'd come and watch him play basketball after school.

This was one morning I didn't want to be alone with you. Alone meant I'd have to tackle your irrational behaviour, somehow get you to see a psychiatrist. I'd brought the subject up after your discharge. You held your hand up like a stop sign, said that psychiatrists were like archeologists. They dug and dug until they found a treasure, and then they left without filling in the hole.

After the others had gone off for the day, I showered and dressed, all the while rehearsing how I'd convince you to get ongoing help. When I came to the kitchen, sunshine, cornflakes, and orange juice coloured the table. You'd even set a place for me.

'I'm going to watch my little bro play basketball this arvo.'
'Good. He'll like that.'

You poured cereal into the bowls, then gave me half the paper, keeping the sporting section. I was searching for a way into the conversation I needed to start up when you opened your hand and I saw the huge blister.

I held your hand still, facing you, so you couldn't help but see the damage. 'Do you remember doing this?'

'Yeah. 'Course.'

'Why did you do it?'

'It doesn't hurt. Not a bit.'

'Why though?'

'A test of strength.'

'I've been awake all night. I can't make sense of it.' I rested my head on the table. 'God, there is no sense to be made!'

'You're talking in riddles, Mum.' You turned the page, pretended to be engrossed in a footy player getting poached.

'No, it's you. It's you who's not making sense. None of us are all-powerful!'

'Jesus is.'

'Well, excluding him.'

'And the devil.'

'Excluding Jesus, the devil, Superman and Batman…Look, Darling, there's this psychiatrist I've heard about…would you talk to him?'

You shook your head. Cupped your hands together, hiding the burn. 'I saw enough shrinks in there to last me a lifetime. Each one of them tried to put my brain in hot water and shrivel it to fit the norm. Whatever that is.'

'Please. For me. Do this for me.' I forced myself not to bow my head. You needed to see my tears.

For a long moment you studied me, unblinking. 'Okay. If it'll help you sleep, sure, why not.' Full of bravado. Then, 'But you'll come with me, won't you?'

The remainder of the day was a good time. We went to Safeway and then called into Shoppingtown to get a few odds and ends, planning to eat Italian. Instead, we bought Chinese takeaway, for you felt too conspicuous in such a large complex. You were fine at the basketball court, though, barracking for your brother. Once home, you opened a bottle of beer and sat in the sun, listening to talkback radio. You got cranky with me because I told you we were all out of beer. It was all out in the garage hidden in the old shopping jeep, a precautionary measure, considering all the drugs you were taking. You never stopped until there was nothing left to drink.

That evening there was laughter from the rumpus room as you three guys played rough-house. My husband was in the family room, reading the paper and sipping on a glass of red. I was carving the leg of lamb when you stood at the steps leading into the kitchen, staring strangely at me. I kept the electric knife moving, juicy slices falling onto the serving plate. Awkwardly, you walked down the two steps. Your body was contorted. I wondered what you were playing at.

'Something's wrong with my neck!' Your large hand seemed to support your throat.

Inwardly I groaned. Please, just let us have this one meal in peace. I turned from the sight of you and stirred the gravy on the hotplate.

'Something's wrong with my neck!'

'Come on, dinner's ready. Call the others.'

You stood there, continuing to push at your face, like you were realigning yourself.

'Dinner's ready everyone!' I called.

Surreptitiously, I watched you as we ate. Your mannerisms were stilted, stiff. Whenever you lifted the fork to your mouth, it was as if each time you had to re-learn how to bend your arm. My husband was going on about the high-roller of a client he'd just snared, while your brothers talked over each other about whose turn it was to mow the lawns. Didn't they see? Did they want not to see? My teeth were so tightly clenched, the fork kept colliding with them.

When you walked away from the table, you looked as if you were two halves; torso jutting to the right side of your legs. You tried to realign your body by leaning back. This only served to exaggerate your weird line, reminding me of a Lego tower, the top block out of sync with the bottom. You managed to sit on the carpeted steps. 'I can't stand this fucking pain. I want to go to hospital. And they'll need to do millions of tests to find out what's wrong.' Your hands covered your face.

I knelt beside you. 'What is wrong?'

You forced a laugh, one I didn't recognise.

'What's wrong, Darling?' I didn't want to know.

'What's what?' You peeped through splayed fingers.

Finally, the others noticed something was amiss. 'What's wrong, what's wrong?' they echoed each other.

I didn't want to be the one to take you to hospital. I wanted to stand at the kitchen sink, squeeze dishwashing liquid into the water, get a good lather up, then wash the glasses, followed by the cutlery, rub the plates until they were squeaky clean, scour the saucepans, wipe the hotplates, benches and table, check the freezer for what to have for dinner tomorrow, make the sandwiches for school lunches, adjust the venetians…

As expected, Casualty was full of waiting people. I led you to a seat welded to a row of seats, then went to the glassed cubicle where I rattled off answers to the nurse's questions.

'Which one's your son?' She peered over my shoulder.

Not wanting you to feel uncomfortable at being pointed out, I said without turning, 'The one on the seat near the vending machine.' The nurse's stern expression seemed to melt. I looked to where she was looking – at a boy with Down's Syndrome who had a perpetual smile. 'No. The one in the red T-shirt.' I nodded in your direction. You stood and walked your crooked body towards me.

'I can't wait. I'm starting to spin out!' you shouted. Your torso looked more off-centre the longer I stared. The nurse didn't bat an eyelid as she promised to hurry you through. Appeased, you returned to your seat.

Suddenly it was me who was spinning out. My words tumbled into each other as I told the nurse, 'It could be marijuana.

Or medication. He's been in a psych hospital. Came out two weeks ago, and…' As I prattled on, she nodded her head over and over, then told me there were four patients with chest pains who needed to be seen first.

You wanted a cup of hot chocolate from the vending machine. I gave you the money. You forgot to insert a plastic cup under the spout. Water splashed onto the chequered floor. I didn't give a damn. About the mess, or the people who stared at you more than at the Down's Syndrome boy.

Eventually we were shown to a curtained cubicle. You lay on the trolley. Silver stars were clustered on the ceiling. On the side table was your admittance sheet. Normally I don't snoop, but this time I felt I had a right. There was nothing, not a word about how lost you were, how frightened I was for you. Just your name, age, health care number and the reason for admittance – 'Stiffness of body', not a word of what I confided to the sister.

Then followed an interminable period of waiting. You either dozed, or drank copious amounts of water from the drinking fountain in the hallway.

'What's made you so thirsty?' I asked.

'I'm just trying to wash the pain away.'

I took the stress tools from my bag. Dealt a game of Patience. Again dealt the same game, sometimes called Solitude. I was musing on how stupid to have different names for the same thing when you said, 'Remember that time…'

I didn't answer, remembering too many times.

'…that time when you tried to get some culture into me? It was one of those free concerts in the park things. I was that sure of being bored, I even took along a 'Phantom' comic. Anyway, the harmony of it all blew me away. I couldn't fathom how all those musos could make the same music at the same time with different instruments. I asked you how they did it.'

'What did I say?'

'Something about it being like map reading. That they

followed symbols on a page and ended up at the same place. And I imagined that's what the world was like – all these different people making the same sound.'

I wondered where this was going. I didn't have long to wonder, for then you said:

'I can't remember the exact moment, but years later I realised I couldn't make that sound.'

'We all walk to a different tune, Son.'

'I don't think anybody walks to mine. They'd have to be running.'

I gathered the cards into a deck. I couldn't stand this anymore, you feeling so isolated from the mainstream. I laid my head on my arms and said a silent prayer to anyone who was listening. The Memory Magician must have been on my wavelength.

'Talking about music,' I said, sitting up straight, 'did I ever tell you that time about the waltz? Well, I was in bed. There I am all snuggled up with a good book, when I hear this waltz. Where could it be coming from? Your stepfather is snoring beside me. My youngest has been asleep for yonks. Your brother is having a shower. No radio in the bathroom. I checked the bedside radio. That was definitely off. Couldn't be the neighbour; it was the middle of winter and the windows were closed. Anyway, the music was so close. Then it stopped and I went back to reading. There it was again, a beautiful waltz. The sound hardly discernible. I yawned and the sound got louder. I closed my mouth. The waltz was silenced. I partly opened my mouth. There it was! Opened wide. Louder now! Closed it again. At this point your brother came in from the bathroom to kiss me goodnight. 'You're not going to believe this,' I said, 'but I've got a radio station coming out of my mouth.' He looked at me as though I was a Martian. 'Truly. Come close.' He began to lower his head to my mouth but before he could hear the waltz, he took off like a shot. Don't blame him, I suppose. It does sound bizarre, doesn't it?'

'Nope.' You shook your head as though you picked up AM and FM all day, every day.

'I wanted someone else to hear it too, so I woke your step-father. He thought I was dreaming when I told him I was picking up a radio station in my mouth. Of course, by the time he was fully awake, the waltz was finished.'

'The signal must've got weaker all of a sudden,' you said.

'Anyway, the next morning they all couldn't stop laughing at me, so I rang Dad, him being an engineer, and asked was it possible for a large silver filling to pick up a radio station?'

'Yeah, course it is,' you said.

'Dad told me it wasn't possible. He thought I was having him on at first.'

'Just because it hasn't happened to him, doesn't mean it can't happen.'

'My thoughts exactly.'

'You should ring ScienceWorks or something like that. They'll tell you.'

Just then the doctor appeared. She studied your admittance sheet and began the usual questions. How many cigarettes a day did you smoke? Eight. Did you drink alcohol? Nah, only a social drinker. Did you take drugs? Nah. Then she asked: 'Are you allergic to anything?'

'Tomatoes,' you said, looking pleased with your prompt recall.

I laughed so hard I wet my pants. The doctor shared a secret smile with me.

'I meant with regard to medication. Are you allergic to any medication?'

'Like I said, just tomatoes.'

'He's taking medication at the moment,' I managed to say.

'And what's that?' she said.

I produced the tablets I'd had the foresight to bring with me. The doctor made a thorough check of your reflexes, moved your limbs backwards and forwards, got you to bend and straighten your back. You seemed to enjoy the attention.

'Sorry about the discoloured socks,' you said, as she tapped the soles of your feet. 'Blue from my moccasins. Had to wash them. My moccasins. They stank. Mum reckoned they didn't. You can never be too sure, though. Never know what's hiding in the furry bits.'

As she made notes on the admittance sheet, you said, 'Can't understand why I'm like this. I'm so fit. Do weights all the time.'

'I think the spasms are probably caused by the medication you're on.' She glanced at her watch. 'You can take extra Cogentan to settle them down.' As you pulled the jumper over your head, she said to me, 'Psych services are only open during the day. Come in tomorrow morning if you feel the need. Better still get in touch with his psychiatrist. Apart from that…'

'I know, call in during office hours. Only get sick during office hours!'

I followed you out of Casualty, astounded at how straight the Lego tower now was.

'That doc was a good sort, wasn't she?' you said, as we walked up the steep hill to the car. 'Wouldn't mind going into hospital with her looking after me.'

Chapter 13

––

It was an ordinary Saturday of shopping, cleaning, then sitting down to crusty bread rolls filled with smoked tuna, and organic tomatoes. I ate lunch under the shade of the grapevine, legs stretched to catch the sun, newspaper spread before me, a bowl of cherries stopping the northerly from blowing headlines into the pool.

The massive shadow thrown by the ornamental grape vine brought back childhood memories of helping the Italian neighbour stomp his grapes into a pulp for vino. My husband hadn't wanted the mess of fallen grapes being trod into our house so I planted an ornamental – a neutered vine. Spring sees the confused vine shedding impotent seeds.

It was the middle of the afternoon. The wind blew hard, and the green seeds came adrift, covering me, and the patio, like mouldy confetti. Still I sat there, enjoying the wind's warmth. I slipped off my sandals, wiggled my toes. Age shows first on toenails. They get so thick and hard, you almost need secateurs to cut them, instead of the nail scissors I was using. The cats were dodging the calcified missiles when the phone rang.

'I'm not getting it!' I called, forgetting for the moment that it was cricket season and so I was home alone. When I did answer the phone, it was you.

'What's up?' I asked, taking the hands-free out to the sunshine.

In a voice devoid of emotion, you said, 'I'm coming across this afternoon.'

'Great. What time?'

'I have to come across.'

'Yeah, fine.'

'I have to come across to kill you.'

'What did you say?'

'I am going to kill you.'

I was suffocating – heart racing, lungs bursting.

'Did you hear me? I have to kill you.'

'Why?' I managed to say.

'Because I've received the message.'

'Where are you?'

'At Nan's.'

'Is she there?'

'Nah.'

'Is anyone there?'

'I have to do this. He said I must.'

'Who said, Darling?' Now it was me who sounded devoid of emotion.

'Jesus.'

'Right. And why would he want you to kill me?'

'Because all my troubles are because of you.'

My legs gave way, I sat down. No hope of running from this, even if I'd wanted to.

'So,' you continued, 'that's why I have to kill you.'

'Come on, you don't mean that,' I cajoled, knowing that you did.

'I have to. He told me.'

This isn't my son. This is the illness. Over and over I reinforced these words to myself as you spewed your mantra of death. Always, when your illness invaded your self, I gently spoke of my reality, trying to get you to read my compass. This time, though, your crippling words spoke not to my intellect, but my heart.

'How dare you! How dare you speak to me like that! I gave birth to you, I'm your mother! How dare you threaten me!'

My anger was real, and not engineered to confront you, for I was mightily scared.

'But I have to do what Jesus says.'

'Jesus' father taught us all to love and honour our parents. He would have taught the same to Jesus, and so I don't think it's Him who's talking to you.'

'It is Him.' The emptiness in your voice scared me more than your words.

'It's the devil, my son. It's the devil's illness. Do you hear me? It's the devil talking.'

'The devil?'

'Yes.'

'I don't know.'

'Tell me, Darling, have you been taking the medication.'

'Yes.' Uncertainty in your tone.

'Every day?'

'Well, nearly every day.' Then, so softly I had to strain to hear. 'I am going to do it. I'm going to catch the bus and come over and kill you.'

'How will you kill me?'

'He hasn't told me yet.'

'I'm hanging up the phone. When you've settled down you can call me back and we'll have a proper conversation.'

I did just that, disconnected us. Then I wished I hadn't for while I had you on the phone you wouldn't be able to kill me. But you'd never do such a thing. Would you? Occasionally the news carried reports of a schizophrenic running amuck.

I was totally alone. My husband was cheering on the boys at cricket. I locked the doors, windows, even secured the cat door.

A few hours later, my husband found me in the corner of the shower, curled into a ball. He had to prise the phone from my hand. When I was able to tell him about your threat, the look on his face scared me as much as the threat.

'How could he! Right. I've had enough of this.'

'Please, it's not him talking, it's the illness.'

'I don't care what it is.' He dialled the phone.

'Who're you ringing?'

'Your son.'

'Please. Hang up! You'll only make things worse.'

'They couldn't get any worse.'

I grabbed the phone from him, just in time to hear you say hello.

'It's me. Mum.'

Silence.

'How are you feeling?'

'Yeah. Okay. Why?'

'Do you remember what you said to me earlier this afternoon?'

Silence again.

'You said you were going to kill me. That Jesus gave you the message.'

'Did I?'

'You don't remember?'

'I was freaked out. Sorry.'

'So you're not freaked out now?'

'I said I was sorry.'

I wanted to say things like, how could you threaten me like that? What makes a son want to scare his mother into hiding in the corner of the shower? But if I ambushed you with questions, you'd retreat even further. Anyway, I knew the answers. Instead, I said, 'Thank you.' Then, 'Would you like to come over? I could pick you up.' Such an inner sigh of relief when you said no. 'Are you sure?'

'Gotta go.'

'I'll call you later. Is Nan home yet?'

'Yeah. Getting tea.'

'And what are you going to do?'

'Get a six-pack.'

'Bye son, I love you.'

Just before I hung up the phone, you said something.

'What was that?'

'They are all your fault. My problems. They are all your fault.'

I waited twenty minutes till I guessed you'd have gone down the street to the liquor shop, then phoned your Nan. I asked her the same questions I'd asked on so many other occasions, and she gave me the same answers. Was he sleeping well? No. Has there been a sudden weight loss? Yes. Was he drinking more? Yes. And his eyes. Do they look darker, the pupils smaller? I think so.

I wasn't suspicious of drugs. When the sickness took hold last time, your eyes mirrored the chaos inside. Pinpricks of despair.

Together we agreed what to do. When you arrived home, she was to call me, let the phone ring three times, then hang up, the code for me to ring the Crisis Assessment Team.

I heard second-hand what happened next, the way I found out about so much of your life. The CAT team arrived early evening. You'd gotten through the six-pack, and more, which, no doubt lowered your defenses. Yeah, you told the broad-shouldered man who carried a black case, not unlike a doctor's, Yeah, I've been hearing voices. I hear them in the television and on the radio and when I play Crowded House. I try not to listen to them. But I listen to Jesus. He is all-knowing. Yeah, the voices keep me awake. I stopped taking the meds because they weren't helping.

Surprisingly, you readily agreed to go with the man and woman who offered you comfort. You quickly packed essentials into an overnight bag and then hopped into the front seat of their car as if just going on a short trip.

That short trip lasted eight weeks behind the high brick wall, all the time waiting, and watching, while the juggler mixed a reality cocktail, first trying this tablet with that, then these two tablets with these three.

When I look back on that time, I wonder how much your brothers witnessed or understood of what went on behind the façade I erected to protect them, not from you, or your illness, but from my sorrow. It would be easier to give birth to a stillborn than to witness your child crumble, to disintegrate from such a ravaging illness that sets up camp in his mind.

'He just needs to pull himself together,' your father said to me one time when I couldn't avoid having to speak with him about you. 'We all have our problems.' I wasn't surprised at his lack of empathy. Empathy is often absent from onlookers when there's no visible break as evidence of the suffering. If your father had bothered to look into your eyes, really look, he would have seen reflected the internal amputation.

Though you wouldn't allow your brothers to visit you two years ago when you were first hospitalised, this time I decided I knew what was best, and not only for you. They were old enough to come to grips with mental illness. They were last time, too, but I listened to you. As it seemed the illness was to be recurring, it was important they see you, understand you weren't a raving lunatic, just a brave young man fighting a debilitating illness.

On the way to visit you, we stopped to buy the biggest parcel of fish 'n' chips. I parked the car right outside the locked door. The nurse agreed to my request, as long as you stayed in the car.

Heat fogged up the windows as we ate the greasy fries.

'They insisted on seeing you,' I said, aware of how jittery you were, how little you ate.

'Yes, we did,' said middle son.

'I just don't want you coming in there.' You jerked your head towards the building with the potted geraniums at the door. 'It's not healthy.'

'But you're getting better,' said my youngest. 'You're getting much better.'

'Yeah, well…' You leant into the door as if feeling for an escape hatch.

I searched for a safe topic. I wasn't used to my sons being so polite to each other.

'When I was a kid…' I began.

'You mean in the Dark Ages,' said my youngest, giggling.

'The Darkest of Dark,' said middle son, trying to outwit his brother.

'As I was saying, we used to get our fish 'n' chips wrapped in newspaper. We'd take it in turns reading out the headlines.'

'Yeah, yeah,' you said, pretending boredom, 'and in the Dark Ages you used cut up newspapers instead of toilet rolls.'

'You wouldn't be able to read the headlines then,' said middle son.

'No, 'cause they'd be printed on your bum!' said my youngest.

'That's what I miss in there. The newspaper,' you said.

'Why? 'Cause they've got no toilet paper,' said my youngest, getting another fit of the giggles.

You pretended to cuff him on the head, like you so often had. I relaxed.

'I'll order a paper for you then,' I said.

'Nah, don't bother. I'd never get it. Someone'd knock it off. Half the time I sleep anyway.'

'Are you going to shave your hair off this time?' asked middle son.

'Dunno. Depends.'

'I like the way your hair's growing. It's got a kink in it.' Wrong thing to say. As soon as I'd mentioned the natural wave, you kept pulling at it. 'As it gets longer,' I assured you, 'the weight will straighten the kink out.'

'Might wear it in a pony tail.'

'Only poofs wear pony tails!' said middle son.

'Might get it cut then.'

'Don't shave it. You'll look too cold,' said my youngest.

'Can wear a beanie.'

'Yeah, but then you'll look like a crim.'

'You need a haircut!' you said in response.

'Going to get it tipped if Mum lets me.'

'Waste of money. Anyway, then you'll look like a poof!' you said.

It was the best, sitting there, sheltered behind fogged windows, eating the greasy chips, listening to my boys carry on as if there was nothing out of the ordinary. I didn't even grumble when they finger-painted the windows, tried to outdo each other with zany caricatures of The Simpsons.

Suddenly, you became agitated, unable to carry a conversation, eyes darting everywhere.

'Gotta go. They'll be looking for me.'

'Can we come tomorrow?' chorused your brothers.

'Nah. Just sometimes. I'll tell Mum when.'

We watched as you waited to be let inside the building with bars on the windows.

'That was the best picnic ever,' said my youngest, as the door opened and you stepped inside.

'Yes, it was,' I said, staring at the closed door. 'For us, anyway.'

Chapter 14

—-—

'What are they?' asks my husband as I undress for bed. He tentatively touches the blisters on my chest. 'You feel so hot.' He puts his hand on my forehead. 'But you don't seem to have a temperature. Do you feel sick?'

If grief is a sickness, I think, instead say, 'I'm fine. Probably chicken pox, or something.' I know it's not chicken pox. I had them as a kid. In the mirror I can see them on my back, too. Soon I will look like bubbled plastic and everyone will want to pop me. 'Get it checked out,' says my husband, studying my body as I continue to undress.

Over the next few weeks, the blisters dry up. Only to pop out someplace else.

'You need antibiotics,' says FF. 'Either that or a holiday.'

'I've just about finished a course of them. Anyway, I think it's just a virus. When I was a kid I had these warts all over my hands. Mum got me washing up the dishes each night and the warts eventually disappeared.'

'Clever Mum! God, imagine the money we'd make if we could patent that cure-all. Wouldn't the mums of Australia love us!'

'You know what you really need?' says FF when next we catch up. 'You need an acupuncturist.' She goes on to tell me how her cleaning lady had wonky knees and had just about given up trying to fix them when, in desperation, she tried Mr Wong. Now she could run a marathon.

I continue to ignore the eruptions on my skin. But I can't

ignore the recurring dream of air escaping from a gash in a tyre. I'm the tyre and there's no spare to replace me. Whenever the dream has played, I lie awake, worrying who would help you if I wasn't there.

The waiting room needs dusting. The receptionist shows me to a cubicle that has a curtain for a door. I undress to knickers and bra. Lie on the stretcher-like bed, hugging the sheet to my neck. I count the pinholes in the ceiling.

Before long, Mr Wong appears from behind a floral curtain.

'And what is wrong with you, Missie?'

I expose my chest and arms and neck, and wait for him to ask about the blisters. I've rehearsed what I'll say, but he doesn't ask. He doesn't even ask about my medical history. He leaves the room, returning with a small container.

'Your body overheated, Missie,' he tells me, as he inserts fine needles into my fingers and toes. 'Like radiator. Problem is, radiator not enough water. So must let heat out of body.'

I lie there, goose pimples hidden, while my digits interact with Mr Wong.

'You don't cry much, Missie?'

'Not much.'

'Do you yell? No? So how you get rid of sad feelings?'

'I go for long walks.'

'Ah, you just put distance between yourself and sadness, that's all,' he says, as he massages the top of my head.

'Or I eat too much.'

'You silly Missie,' he says, tsk tsking, and suddenly I'm in sixth grade and Mrs McLean is clicking her tongue against her teeth because I talk too much. 'Missie must find way of letting sad devil out.' He massages my ear lobes. 'Hold him in too long and he eats you away.' He goes to my feet and twiddles the needles in my toes. 'Missie must get in touch with who lives inside. You get sad, angry, you must cry or break plates or find space where no sadness lives.'

As he fiddles with my extremities, I wonder if everyone has that space inside them where no-one, nothing, can enter, least of all themselves.

'You Westerners say, no pain no gain.' He smiles, and I'm surprised to see such decayed teeth on a man who practises medicine. 'You sort out problem, and problem sort out you. But first you must find problem that makes body want to jump out of skin. Missie might need to take in her mind a long journey. And then she must stop at all stations on way back.'

'I wouldn't know where to start this journey.'

'You go to beginning and then end. Yes, Missie, the beginning of the end.'

I don't want to go to that place. But if I don't face my demons I'll surely deflate, become as useless as a gashed tyre.

When I force myself to take that journey one afternoon when I'm stuck inside, torrential rain nearly drowning out my thoughts, the neuralgia starts up again. It's the same pain that began hammering inside my cheek that awful time…

You cried when we left. Only three and already life was hurting you. I told you everything would be better, that Mummy and Daddy wouldn't fight anymore.

Driving down the road that would take us to a calmer place, I passed the house where I'd taken refuge the night before. It had happened just on midnight. I'd been at work all day. Picked you up from creche, then we'd visited your uncle in hospital. Managed to fit McDonalds in somewhere between hospital and home. You were overtired. It took an hour to settle you to sleep. Your father had taken to not coming home some nights. I was hoping this would be one of them. I'd just turned off the telly when headlights lit the lounge window. He stumbled inside, flung himself down on the lounge, legs astride like his horse had bolted, leaving him in the saddle.

'Where's my tea?' he shouted.

'I've been out.'

'Where to this time!'

'Visiting my brother in hospital.'

'So, is he gunna live?'

'They're still testing for rheumatic fever.'

'Only old people get that.'

'There's baked beans in the pantry.'

'You can get it.'

'I'm tired. I've got an early meeting tomorrow.'

He stood, towering over me. 'If you were a proper wife you'd make sure there was a meal ready for me.'

Avoiding conflict, I went to get ready for bed. I was brushing my teeth when I heard him go to the fridge, heard the hiss of beer being opened. He stood at the door, sucking on the bottle, watching me. 'Was your old woman at the hospital?'

'Mmmm.' I spat the toothpaste into the basin. I knew why he asked. Over the last few months our verbal fisticuffs had escalated to the point where we didn't hear each other anymore, didn't want to. Recently we had calmly agreed it was time to separate. And that we'd individually take responsibility of telling our parents. I'd delayed telling Mum and Dad, hoping that our marriage would somehow gel again.

It was you, just two nights earlier who forced me to face reality. You'd been asleep for hours. Your father and I were in bed, an arena where now only accusations and recriminations were shared, and this night was no exception. I heard your little voice. 'Stop. Stop. It hurts.' I turned on the lamp. There you stood, holding your dummy and clutching teddy. You didn't even reach the door handle, yet you'd managed to climb out of the cot with its high railings. I cried, for you had to find your way in the dark.

'So,' he said, in a menacing voice. 'What did you and your old woman talk about?'

'Mum asked where you were. I told her I hardly knew these

days. In fact, I told her the only thing I was sure of was we were separating.'

Owl eyes stared. 'You bitch. Couldn't wait to tell her, could you.'

'It's what we agreed.'

When I looked in the mirror, he wasn't there. There was a noise from the spare bedroom. I knew it was from that room because he never went to check on you when you were sleeping. That noise again. Like a deadbolt opening and closing. My grandfather made that noise just before he shot a rabbit. Suddenly my husband was in the mirror, standing just off-centre, smirking. The bottle of beer in one hand, a rifle in the other. Slowly, very slowly, he raised the rifle till it was pointing at me. The bathroom had two exits. I couldn't run to you asleep in the cot. That would only lead him to you. I ran through the bedroom, out the front door. My pounding footsteps didn't muffle his.

Only the one light at the bottom of the street. I was flying through the air. Then I was banging on the neighbour's door. 'Close it, quick!' I said as they let me in. 'He's chasing me with a gun. My husband. He has a rifle!'

They bolted the door. Closed the drapes. We stood in the lounge beside the entrance hall. Five, ten minutes, whispering, what do you want to do? Ring the police? Your father? No, not my father. Don't want to worry him, he's recovering from open-heart surgery. And not the police. The shame of calling the police.

Then gentle knocking. No gun in his hand now.

'I didn't mean anything. I just had too much to drink. I wouldn't hurt her.'

An hour of sitting around the neighbour's kitchen table, my husband consuming cup after cup of black coffee. Him so contrite and believable. 'I just hit the booze too hard.' All the while he slurped on the coffee, I prayed you were still sleeping safe in the cot. I wanted to run home. Alone. Escape with you. No escape tonight. Such action would only endanger you. Lead his anger to both of us.

'So what do you want to do?' asked the neighbour of me. 'You can sleep here, if you want to.'

'It's okay. I'll be all right.' I had no choice. I had to go back, for you were there.

As soon as we stepped off the neighbour's porch, they closed the door. I walked a few steps behind him. He kept turning, wanting me to catch up. I wondered as we neared each bush if it would be my last step. That bush, or that bush could conceal the rifle. No, never again would I catch up with him.

I put a chair against the handle of your bedroom door. All night I sat in that chair. You slept unaware, while I stayed awake, all too aware. When night turned itself inside out, letting the sun creep over the windowsill, I was still listening, and thinking of how your father, when a teenager, forced a kitten into a milk bottle and left it in the sun to die. The time he raised his fist to me, at the last minute directing it at the wall, punching a hole in the plaster instead of me. As the bile rose in my gullet, the bitter list in my head grew and grew.

We made the best of things, you and I, living in a third floor flat, flanked by higher matchbox flats that kept the sun at bay. The only furniture, your bed, chest of drawers and the fridge so your food wouldn't go rancid. I could have taken more. Half of everything, at least, but I preferred to sleep and eat on the floor, unwilling to bring with me the odour of bad memories.

Then began what was to be the pattern for more than ten years. Your father's fortnightly weekend access. Sometimes he took you to his mother's – a built-in-babysitter. But too many times he took you away for weekends with his mates, roughing it by the Murray River. Weekends when I couldn't stop the image of you falling into the murky water, wild currents sucking you to nowhere.

Then the night you weren't home at the appointed time of eight-o'clock. As each hour passed, I waited for the knock on the door, waited for a policeman to tell me there'd been an accident. I paced from the stairwell to the balcony. If I wasn't pacing, I sat in the beanbag, staring at your muddied handprint on the wall.

There's a knock on the door. I don't want to answer it. Don't want to know. Slowly I open the door, and there you are! Tears streak the dust on your face. I smell alcohol, see his bloodshot eyes. In one movement, I take you in my arms and try to kick the door shut, but I'm not quick enough. Your father pushes his way in, stands there, trying to stay balanced. He has that owl look again. I back down the hallway, you in my arms.

'Get him to bed,' he says, voice full of threat.

'I'll bathe him first. He's putrid.'

'Don't bother with the bath. Get him to bed. I'll wait for you out here.'

Behind the closed bedroom door I put teddy bear pyjamas over grubby arms and legs. Your hair is stiff, like it's been combed with egg-whites. I tuck you beneath the clean sheet, pull the blanket up to your neck.

'Tell me the rest of the story,' you say, eyelids already closing.

I kneel beside you. Our story has no end. You and I make it up as we go along.

'The kangaroo bit,' you say, eyes closed now.

And I tell you how the kangaroo shows the boy how to survive in the bush, until one day, a hunter corners the kangaroo and the boy pushes the hunter into a rabbit hole.

'What happened then?' you mumble.

'Well, then the kangaroo puts the brave little boy into his pouch and they hop, hop...'

The door slams open. 'Hurry up. Get out here!'

Your eyes open wide, short arms stretching for me.

'Get out here!'

I grab your little body to me, ashamed I'm using you as a shield.

'You know what I want. Get out here.'

'Please go.'

'If you don't give me what I want, I'll do something,' he snarls. Dingo eyes replace owl eyes. Dingo eyes looking at you.

'Please. Just give me a few minutes.'

I put you back to bed. You try so hard to keep your eyes open, and all the while they close, your eyes never leave mine. I hum you to sleep. Close tight your door.

He is in the lounge, leaning against the wall fondling his stiff cock. He eyeballs me, tilts his head in the direction of the floor.

'Please, don't do this,' I whisper.

'If you don't get down on that floor like the whore that you are, I swear, I'll go in there and do something to him.'

I lie on the floor. He prises me open. There's a crack in the ceiling that runs from the french doors, up the hallway, till I can't see anymore. My head bangs against the wall as he pummels inside me, stopping only when he shudders. I hear a zip being pulled. Feel the spittle that lands on my face.

He leaves me there, all curled up on the stained carpet. Just like he'd left the kitten in the bottle.

The front door slams.

I deadbolt the door. Go to check on you. The door is ajar. You've pulled the tiny chair to reach the handle. You sit on the floor, arms raised to me. I lift you, hold tight your quivering body, though I can't tell who's clinging to whom. I settle you back to bed. Your breathing is out-of-whack – short, hurried breaths. Eventually you sleep.

The shower runs cold, but still I stand there rubbing myself raw with the soap. Unable to rid myself of his smell.

All week at work, I was unable to concentrate on the upcoming merger and Board meeting. How long were you sitting there and what did you see, hear? I wanted to tell you, Mummy wasn't hurt, that Daddy was just angry. If I pretended that night never happened, you too, might forget.

Over the next few months, every time I saw him, I wanted to have him charged for rape. I wanted someone bigger than me to protect us. But that was the early seventies and spousal rape wasn't a crime.

The next fortnightly visit I waited at the gate to hand you over. 'Could you please have him back by four?'

'Why should I!'

'It's just that he's got a party to go to.'

'I'll try,' he said, grudgingly.

At four on Sunday, I was at the gate, waiting.

When he arrived at five o'clock he said, 'I want to come up.'

I scooped you into my arms. 'Say 'bye to Daddy. We have to hurry to the party now.'

He grabbed you out of my arms. 'I want to come up!'

'Please, don't.' I kept my voice on an even keel, afraid of alarming you.

'I'm not giving him back then. You'll never get him.' He turned and walked away.

I wanted to jump on him, gouge his eyes. Instead, I stood there, pretending a confident smile as you looked from your father to me.

For an hour I sat by the phone, wondering if he had driven into the bush and taken you from me forever. I was just about to pick up the receiver to call the police when the phone rang.

'If you want him back, I'm outside the cop shop, just a block away.'

He knew he had me cornered, scared. That's why he was waiting outside the police station. Daring me to take action. I ran to where you were.

Like Humpty Dumpty, he had you sitting on the brick wall. The backdrop of the blue and white Police sign gave me no comfort. You were licking an ice-cream and clutched a bag of lollies. Your father sat on the fence beside you, smirking. I went up to him, waited for you to be handed down to me.

'Could I please have my son. It's getting late, and he needs to sleep.'

'Pretty please,' he said.

'Pretty please, could I have my son.'

Holding your forearms, he dangled you in the air. I grabbed you to me. There I stood, accepting your offer of a lick of the ice-cream, exclaiming over the too-many lollies, all the time watching him until he drove away from us.

He didn't rape me again. Didn't steal you from me. He had made his point. If he wanted to, he could be in total control. Of me. Of you.

Now, each time I see Mr Wong in his room at the back of the herbal shop, my tears gradually escape. He doesn't say anything about the overflow. Witch doctor that he is, he must know I'm facing the past in order to handle the present.

My last appointment. I dread not forever having Mr Wong to press the buttons that drain me of fear and anger. I always thought if I cried as much as I have been, the crack in the dam would burst and I'd drown. When I told Mr Wong this, he clicked his rotten teeth and said, 'Sometimes, Missy, we have to get ourselves empty before we can be full.'

Chapter 15

——

Between my chenille dressing gown and pink cardigan labelled GAP, hangs your sports jacket that has five pockets – three outside, two inside. Each morning, before I reach for something to wear, I hold its empty sleeve – the right sleeve. 'Got it for ten dollars at the Op Shop. Must've belonged to a toff who had more money than sense!' you said, as you self-consciously stood before me, seeking approval. Some mornings I brush the empty sleeve against my cheek, others I grab the lapels and bury my head where your chest should be. The pockets are empty, though sometimes I search them, just in case.

You wore the jacket to your uncle's birthday bash. That was also the time you first wore glasses. They made you look sophisticated, weren't like you at all, though you didn't always wear them, just when the illness became invasive. They were an armour of sorts, I suppose, an impenetrable window, a way of distancing from us.

I took the jacket from your room after the funeral. I took everything from your room immediately after the funeral. Your treasures only filled a fruit box. The box, too, sits in my wardrobe. When I need to hug you, I sit on the faded roses that decorate the doona and lay your treasures before me. There's a bundle of birthday, Christmas, and get well cards. In the battered wallet is your business card, headed 'Man of Action'. In the billfold is a meticulously folded newspaper article with the heading, 'Make Marijuana Legal', and beneath that a photo of the Opposition Leader who wanted to do just that. Old magazines on cricket and

Top Fishing Ideas, comics from your childhood, binoculars, *Turners Four Figure Mathematical Tables*, *Very Best of Crowded House*. In the cash tin with the forced lock is an application to join the Labor Party, fishing hooks, and the special ring that protected you from evil. (Why weren't you wearing it that night?) I pore over the photo album of the two of us, the one I put together. You've added a couple of Polaroid snaps; one of a seedling in a black pot, the other a mature marijuana plant. A before and after. If there's no-one at home I rifle through the things you once held. When I hear the garage door open, I quickly pack everything away till next time. Though I can never pack your love away. It wouldn't fit in the box marked 'Yellow Cling Peaches'.

Yesterday I was doing just that, sifting through your treasures, when the doorbell rang. It was a policeman at my door. Seemed there was a robbery across the road. A break-in. 'Did you see anything, know anything?' he asked.

And I think: No, but there's been a thief in my house. He came during the night. Robbed us of our most precious. He'd been planning for weeks, months, even. While all the time we'd been planning our existence.

'Did you see anything suspicious?'

I knew nothing, saw nothing. Too busy.

'Sometimes,' he said, 'neighbours see something out of the ordinary, but it often doesn't register at the time.'

This stealthy thief crept in through the cracks of love and self-worth and took up residence in my son's mind. Ate away at the laneways and backroads until it came to the crossroad.

'Are you okay?'

And there it smugly sat, biding its time, only speaking when he dared to vacillate. Blaming, egging him on. Deluding him into taking that road away from the junction.

'Look, I'm sorry to bother you. But we have to cover all avenues. What with insurance claims and all...'

No, officer, I haven't made a claim. It wasn't that the premium would increase. More that I'm still trying to work out the cost to us all.

'Is there anyone at home with you? You're very pale.'

'What?' I say, finding my voice. 'Oh, just a virus. Sorry I couldn't be of any help.'

'There's a lot of that going around at the moment.'

I closed the door. Such an apparition in the hall mirror. A dressing-gowned woman with tangled, wet hair. Eyes hollowed from remembrance. It's when she goes to knot the cord at her waist she falls to the polished floor.

I must have escaped into sleep for quite some time for when I stood and again caught sight of myself in the mirror, an indented line ran down my cheek, an imprint from the floorboard. The cord around my waist had again come loose. I wished that never again would I have to tie a knot. The cord dragged on the ground as I went to the kitchen to make a cup of tea. 'A nice cup of tea will make everything much brighter.' That's what my old Gran used to say. And 'Never trouble trouble till trouble troubles you.' It's hard not to be troubled when doing things like pulling the tie on a rubbish bag, putting on a necklace, knotting shoelaces, only illuminate your last moments. Scores in my every cell the depth of that blackness.

Now, I'm again sitting on the faded roses that have no thorns. The photos have gone an orangey colour. I didn't have the negatives. They'd been lost in the many moves. The album has five empty pages. Did you understand, truly understand how you were knotting a root of your family tree? Did you stop to think? So easily snuffing generations of hope. A past made redundant. In the dead of night you stole, two, three, maybe four less grandchildren to shade me in old age. Tomorrow's never now.

In photos I confuse you with your brother. That likeness scares me. But appearances can be deceptive. No, I must not deceive myself, it can happen to any one of us. And it did…

Grandfather – all those years in that chair, just a pipe, and jam tin for a spittoon.

Nephew – departed on a heroin track.

Niece – her head in the oven. Underdone.

Cousin – on a mountain, lost in the clouds.

Yet another being saved in the nick of time, as he more than nicked himself.

And there's you, my son.

While outside my bedroom window an azalea withers. Though not from disease, but purely lack of water, or so the nurseryman tells me

See how the bitterness grows in me. An apricot tree in exchange for a family tree.

I store the box high in the wardrobe, then crawl beneath the doona. This gnawing inside me eats a canyon so deep no amount of fill will replenish. This gnawing inside me. What if it stops? I must keep on feeling for while I do, you'll never die.

The dream wakes me. I dreamt of ladders. Borrowing, hiring extensions to reach you. When I entered the blackness, stars my streetlights, frantically I tried to climb but the rungs disintegrated and I was afraid, so very afraid I'd never be able to reach you. Like in a childhood dream where I ran in the same place, terrified of what was behind me. Was it like that for you? Running on the spot until the fear caught up?

When my family arrive home, I'm peeling vegies, boiling the kettle, and assuring the cats they'll be fed soon. Juggling is something I'm good at. Juggling keeps me focused. I'm glad my family are home. I welcome their noise. Once I used to enjoy my own company. Now there's a deathly quiet in solitude that seeps into my soul leaving me bereft. A cobweb of dread that invisibly clutches.

'So what've you been doing today?' asks my husband over dinner.

'This and that.' I search for something to define my day, something I won't have to substantiate. 'Cleaning out cupboards. Boring stuff.' I hate lying but he's already worried about my state of mind, as he puts it. It only adds to your depression, he'd recently told me when he came upon me crying into the fruit box.

Last thing at night, after I've called the cats inside, turned the heating off, deadlocked the front door, and kissed my boys goodnight, I go the wardrobe and breathe in your smell.

I worry that when I die the sports jacket will be turfed, given to the Salvos or something. It must hang in the wardrobe of someone who loved you, and when they are dead, it must hang in the wardrobe of someone who would love you if they'd only known you.

At work, yet another raffle to raise money to enhance the residents' facility. This time, a multicoloured clown made by the craft ladies who meet every Tuesday afternoon. Two for a dollar, the sign says. Someone has put a screw in the arch that leads to my office. A chain dangles from the screw. The clown is affixed to the chain. And there it hangs. Sometimes swinging from the draught. My first inclination was to take the clown off the chain, instead sit it on the counter, no matter that it would flop and not be shown to its advantage. I resisted, continue to resist, for I must go with the flow of life. A flow that will inexorably contain you, your image.

I sit at the computer and concentrate on the screen. But no roster, menu or confirmation letter for residency can divert me from the dangling shadow I can't help but see from the corner of my eye. The raffle will be drawn at the end of the month. Days and days of seeing you dangle from the bottlebrush. Did you occasionally circle as the clown does? Or did your weight keep you centred?

So many times I reach out, turn the clown to face the right way. Is there a right way to face when you are hanging? Rude to have your back to the crowd. You won't sell many raffle tickets that way!

Yesterday, a courier delivered twelve dozen boxes of incontinence pads. As I was signing the delivery docket, he said, 'Shit. This is macabre.' He was looking at the clown. 'Must give you nightmares,' he said staring at me. Was the association between the clown and you so apparent on my face? 'It's a beautiful clown,' I said. 'A hanging,' he said. A colleague was in my office at the time. I felt her anguish for me.

If I take the clown off the chain, I will be admitting defeat. But defeat of what? Death is the most defeatist of them all. Waving a white flag is not my style. Chin up, look straight ahead, listen to the orders of command. That is what I learnt in the army. By the right...By the left...Eyes straight ahead! Commands that keep a soldier focused. Commands that keep me from dangling like the clown.

As my rapid-fire fingers tap the keyboard, replacing Chocolate Mousse with Rhubarb Pie (only because the rhubarb in the residents' vegie garden needs to be picked), I think I can withstand the hanging clown if I attach a thread to its limbs. If a courier should again exclaim its macabreness, I can deftly pull the strings and mimic a Punch or Judy. Thus cancelling out, for working time at least, the image of your death by hanging.

When I have finished the menu, I start on the roster, replacing those on the sick list with healthy workers. Mary replaces Jane for the kitchen shift; Lynda replaces Meg for the supervisors' evening shift; Priscilla replaces John for the cleaning shift. As I create a workable roster, I close my left eye so I can't see the dangling clown. Working with a wink, instead of dying with a wink.

'What's wrong with your eye?' asks a colleague, as she feeds paper into the fax machine.

'Nothing.'

'Why have you got it closed, then?'

'I can see better that way.'

She stands there, waiting for the machine to spit out the paper.

I open the eye. Quickly close it. Tell myself, shadows are just that. A pretence. Shadows can be anything you want them to be. As a kid I'd lie in bed waiting for Dad to come and kiss me goodnight, and while I waited for the kiss that would signify the end of a day, promise of another, I'd link my thumbs and make moving shadows on the wall – a butterfly, an elephant, a sunflower even. If I'd wanted, I could've made horrible shadows, a ghost, the devil even. Shadows are what you make them.

'I've got some eye drops if it's itchy,' says my colleague, as she stamps the paper with the word, Faxed.

'Truly, I'm fine.'

She looks at me as though I'm not.

I will keep both eyes open. The shadow that jiggles every time the automatic doors open, I will make out as something other than you. When next a visitor enters the building, I will imagine the clown is a fern, trembling in the breeze.

I concentrate on the illuminated screen as I compose a thankyou note to a business that has kindly donated a dinner-for-two for the coming Mother's Day raffle. I touch-type so am able to close both eyes. This gives me some respite, even if momentarily.

When the menu and roster and correspondence are finished, it's the end of the day. I pull the security screen on my office and turn the lock. My elbow knocks the clown, and it starts up its crazy dance of death.

At home, I park the car on the road. Once my husband and I had use of the double garage. But now your brothers each have a car. It was me that offered to give them the use of the garage. After all, their cars are better than ours!

You never had a car. You never had lots of things. Though you did have your driver's licence…

You'd arrived for the weekend with a backpack full of beer, looking as proud as if you'd conquered Mt Everest.

'Mum, I did it. I got my licence.'

'Good on you! Well done!' I hugged you as tight as you'd let me.

'Second go, but anyway…'

'That's brilliant. I am so proud of you.'

You stacked the beer into the fridge. Told me how nervous you were doing the computer test. How you thought you would've failed the driving test because you'd not given way to the right. That the instructor must've felt sorry for you.

'Rubbish! They're so strict on the test. You wouldn't have passed unless you'd been good enough.'

You shrugged away my confidence. 'Don't tell the others, will you? I want to surprise them. Sort of, just get in the driver's seat when we're going out somewhere and scare the shit out of them.'

'Forget the beer,' I said, 'this deserves champagne!' I turned off the oven. Bugger the roast. I'd camouflage the soggy potatoes with gravy.

As we drove towards the liquor shop, I pulled to the side of the road. 'Would you like to drive?'

'Nah. It's okay.'

'Go on. I trust you.'

'Another time.'

There never was another time.

At home, we sipped on champagne as I made double the usual quantity of gravy. Rather, I sipped, you guzzled.

And there we were, all five of us sitting around the table eating a drowned-in-gravy roast. You seemingly sober as flat lemonade, me tipsy, wanting to shout to my family your achievement. I knew how much effort the test took, what a store of self-esteem you had to garner to even apply. Your brothers had so much,

I wanted them to celebrate your success.

Then the usual homecoming question from my husband to you. 'So, what are you doing about getting a job?'

'I go down to the dole office three times a week,' you said, eyes on your plate. 'Check the board for jobs. There's never much there.'

I could sense your discomfit, imagined you felt as though the Gestapo was on the prowl.

'You'll feel much better in yourself if you get a job,' said my husband. 'We all need something to get up for. I can think of nothing worse than waking up and having no direction.'

You said nothing, retreating into the safety of your shell.

I waited till we were in bed, the usual place for recriminations. 'You shouldn't go on at him about getting a job. He's doing his best.'

'I don't think he's doing anything.'

'He's got an illness. Try to understand…'

'I just think that if he had a job, a lot of his problems would disappear.'

'Try to understand that pressure of any sort can set him off again. Stress can accelerate the illness, cause it to reappear.'

'He needs to…'

'He told me just this week of this recurring dream he has. A cocky pecks at the skin on his arm and he can't shrug it off. And all the while the cocky strips the bone it says, "What a fucking useless bastard you are".'

'Just goes to show how he needs to feel normal.'

'Well, there's no hope of that if you keep going on at him about how he doesn't fit society's template!'

'I only want what's best for him.'

What's best for us, I think. Whatever makes us feel comfortable. Get him to fit the mould of our circle – a productive lot of go-getters who keep themselves busy, busy, and that way don't have time to examine their lives, fearful the revelation would be as uncomfortable as wearing shoes two sizes too small. How very difficult it must be not to fit the template. Made more difficult when others tag you as a dole bludger. That's something you're not. When you were discharged from hospital, the social worker had an application form filled out for you to sign.

'What's this?' you asked, peering at the small print.

'It's to claim a Disability Pension.'

'I don't want that.'

'You're eligible.'

'I'm not disabled.'

The Disability Pension paid more than the dole. You knew that. Still, you refused to be branded.

Arriving home one night, I realise daylight saving has started. Spring too, has sprung without me realising, for bees hover over new colours that dot the garden. I do the usual routine of bending to scratch Grey Cat's back and check for mail. It's as I walk up the brick driveway that I stop short at what's blooming red in the neighbour's garden.

That night, I wait till my family have been asleep for hours. Slowly, slowly, I slide out of bed and slip my feet into slippers strategically placed. Down the hallway to the family room, then two steps down to the next level. The sliding door glides silently. The cats don't stir from the couch. Slow, short steps in case the hose hasn't been rewound. I arm myself with the yellow-handled tool I'd hidden behind the rubbish bin.

The neighbour's house is in darkness. As I cross their lawn, the porch sensor light comes on. I crouch beside a tree until the light goes off. The sound of sawing is loud. Still, I don't slow the backwards and forwards rhythm. I wish it were storming, so I could hide within its noise. A car cruises by. I stop, start again when the headlights disappear. The trunk of the bush leans away from me, bottlebrush flowers drape the ground. I saw and saw until the trunk is severed.

And then I wake from yet another nightmare.

Chapter 16

The anniversary must be soon, they say, with soft smiles, eyes downcast.

I start to panic. What is expected of me? A torrent of tears so swift I'll come adrift, or, fists flailing at the Wailing Wall. Even a mute grief which sends me screaming? But if I do none of these things, will they think heartless, no-good mother? Or will they silently watch, sure that if not this anniversary, then I will go under the next.

Paper, silver, gold rubies. What shall I give you for this our First Anniversary? The ashes that were my heart? Sapphires, emeralds, diamonds, opals. No, there aren't enough gems for anniversaries that reach into eternity...though you did score an eternity ring around your neck.

It's near midnight. My husband sleeps on the chair fully reclined. I'm upright on the matching chair. The boys have gone to bed, bored with the documentary that drones in the background. We can never forget tomorrow, not even if we want to. Remembrance Day. The eleventh day of the eleventh month, the day the country stops for a minute at eleven o'clock to remember those who died fighting for freedom, the day you now share with so many others.

Near midnight, and I teeter on the cusp of the day you lived and the day you died. There is no grandfather clock to mournfully strike twelve times – just a discernable tick, tick, ticking from the railway clock on the wall.

The hands meet at the top.

And now it is a year since you left us numbed with grief,

angry that death crooked its dirty finger, promising you what? A soothing sleep, nestled forever in a valley green? Even relief for those left behind?

I fucking taught you about stranger danger, and death is the most dangerous stranger of all!

My husband wakes, tries to focus on the crawling ants shown on the documentary channel. I pretend to sleep. This day of days is a time for silence. I wish the running thoughts that besiege me will trip over, knocking themselves out. The persistent ants fade to nothing, and before long we're privy to a program on open-heart surgery. While my husband snores, I sigh at my loss, gasp at your absence, then somehow go back to breathing because something keeps winding my clock.

The phone rings. My husband wakes, tries to centre himself. I can't move to stop the shrill ring that goes on and on.

'Hello,' he says. Then, 'Yes, I'm coming.'

He strips off his dressing gown, then pyjama pants as he walks up the hall.

'Is it your Dad?' I ask, as I pick up his scattered clothes.

He nods. Concentrates pulling on Bali shorts, then, 'He's gone.'

'I'm coming with you.' Quickly I dress in what I've been wearing that day.

The old man has been dying for weeks now. Weak and yellowed like a jaundiced baby. When I sat with him as he lay spread-eagled on the bed, I was impatient with his whining and crying. Still, I rubbed his arm and told him not to be afraid, that it was his time to rest, that he'd had a long life. 'Go gently,' I said, as he railed at death.

The old man's family tip-toed around the subject of his death. One day I went to his good wife who now carried a hanky with her broom. 'Talk to him about dying,' I said. 'Don't avoid it. He knows.'

'Oh, I do, I do,' she said, blowing her nose and sweeping. 'I tell him we are not all born at the same time and so we can't go together. And that he has to go to make room for the young.'

Swiftly she swept the clean floor while I stood there, face burning, throat aching from holding back what I wanted to say. I retreated to the back yard and stood beneath the lemon tree. I'd counted fifty-seven lemons when my husband came looking for me.

'Are you okay?'

'No.'

'What's up?'

'How dare your father whinge and cry. So ungrateful.' I grabbed the awning stick that was always beside the tree and hit at the lemons. Hit them so hard they split open before falling to the ground.

He took the stick from me, leant it against the garage wall. 'What happened in there?'

'Your mother told him it was his turn to die, that he had to make way for the young ones.'

'Makes sense.'

'But that means my son's early death gave your father overtime. And he's still fucking ungrateful.' Like a desperate soccer player, I kicked the lemons in all directions.

My husband stood there, staring at me, trying to see what he couldn't.

Can it be only three days since I destroyed those lemons? We pull up outside the triple-fronted, brick veneer house. 'What time did your father die?'

'Tante said he was comfortable when she checked on him at eleven thirty, but ten minutes later he wasn't breathing.'

I'm glad for today, Remembrance Day, is your day, and your day only.

The house is lit up like it's waiting for guests. I follow my husband up the carpeted hallway that, until just a few years ago, we had to take our shoes off before walking its length.

I stare down at the dead man who looks harmless enough now. The four lengths of hair that covered his baldness have slipped to the side. A circle of hair surrounds the pink skin and from where I stand at the headboard, his head could be a baby crowning at birth.

I leave my husband, his sister and mother to say their final goodbye. Before going outside to direct the car from the funeral home, I stand in the hallway and listen to the sound of muffled weeping, the sound of the living supporting each other, crying for themselves.

When the old man has been bagged and taken away, we leave Mutti with the many women who have shared the nursing. Already they have begun scrubbing the room, trying to exorcise the death smell with Pine-O-Cleen.

Again, death silences us as we drive home, always this silence immediately following death, a silence more respectful than prayer. If it were forty years ago, there'd be the clinking of bottles as milk was delivered to the houses with dark windows. But it's not forty years ago when everything was slow and easy. It's now, this awful time when grief keeps rearing its head as death calls for an encore. I place a hand on my husband's leg, like I did when we were courting. I know what he is feeling, and I want to tell him not to allow grief to enter, not to open the door to a presence that gnaws and gnaws and gnaws until you become who you aren't. If you do open that door, one day you will break in half, and they will see the heart-rot; the putrefaction of petrified love. Do not open the door.

My husband is caught up in his father's funeral arrangements and I'm left alone on this anniversary day. When the boys are at their Omi's, I start searching, for what I don't know. In the spare room, on the shelf that holds odds and sods from long ago, I leaf through diaries of my teenage years. There are no words about you for you were still waiting to be born. In a ruled exercise book, where the word 'Algebra' has been crossed out, replaced with 'Favourites', are the recipes I cut out from magazines. Curried Sausages, Beef Florentine, Brandy Snaps, Coq Au Vin, Never Fail Pavlova. And then I find it! What I have been searching for, though not even remembering its existence. Between Special Fried Rice and Scalloped Potatoes lies a jewel on a tattered page.

In childish scrawl:

I love

You

Mum

500

Ah, your anniversary gift to me. And I remember the sparring of love words:

Do you know how much I love you? One million dollars worth!
But Mum, I love you more than that.
How much more?
Outside the world and into the universe.

I keep searching until I come across a leather-bound book. A long-ago birthday present from my mother. I flick from the back page. Blank, blank, and more blanks. Yes! The first two pages have precise, tiny writing. Words so cramped I need my glasses to read them.

February 1970:
I have a son! A beautiful son. He has a crooked smile, and a stubborn cowlick. And he hardly sleeps. Being a mother is hard work. Getting the baby clothes ready, and buying the pram was like playing at dolls. Being a mother is like not having time to go out and play. When my baby gets a sleeping rhythm perhaps then I'll get to read a book!

Then nothing, until:

November 1975:
My son is 6, and it's that many years till I've written in this book.

There certainly hasn't been time for play! Like me, he has a temper but overcomes his outbursts very quickly. First school report this week. His teacher was in my form at high school. We never got on. At the interview she told me my son has a behavioural problem, in that he finds it hard to concentrate for any length of time and so tends to distract the class. She went on to add that all the children in the class who came from single parent families had the same problem! Still, I talked this over with our doctor and he advised me to go on my own intuition. 'If your son is good at home, don't worry.' So, I'm not.

March 1976:
The man I have married is a wonderful stepfather to my son. They are real mates – for hours playing cricket in the street, or kicking a football.

His latest school report states that, scholastically, he's doing better, and no longer has a behavioural problem, though he tends to be a bit of a loner.

And then no more entries. Probably because I became immersed in nappies and sterilising bottles once again.

I read the entries over and over. Not sleeping. Behavioural problem. Loner. Were these signs something was already amiss in your head?

But I did sense, just two or three years later that something wasn't quite right. That was the time I was into tapestries, and would spend all my sitting down time pushing a needle in and out of the square piece of hessian. With each pattern came the thread, just enough, in various colours to complete the picture. One Saturday morning, I made you breakfast and then you went outside to ride the bike. I went downstairs to the laundry and as I passed the corner where the light was brightest, on the floor were hundreds of short threads. You admitted cutting the threads. Because you were angry, you said, but didn't know why. I knew how debilitating bottled anger could be, and so we saw a counsellor. At the end of four sessions, the counsellor asked you to wait outside. 'He's a normal, well adjusted, happy little boy,' she told us. And she produced the picture you'd drawn of a house with smoke spiraling out of the chimney, flowers and trees, and stick figures of mum and stepdad and baby brother. Other drawings of your grandparents and uncles. I didn't realise till studying the pictures, some months later, in none of the drawings had you depicted your father.

When you were seventeen, had left school and unemployed, the gnawing sense of something not quite right preyed on me. Nothing I could put my finger on, just an uneasy sense. Another assessment, this time by a Youth Counsellor. Again, apart from you needing a focus, a glowing report that made me think I was the one in need of assessment; I was seeing what wasn't there.

I put the leather-bound book in the beauty case where I store remnants of you.

The next day, I'm clawing my way back from the blackness of the anniversary. Your death's still sharp, for me, for everyone, though some seem blunted by it. Me, too, sometimes. Blunt is when I think I should feel more; sharp is when I can feel no more.

Some days 'It', your death, bangs against me reaching into every organ, trying to shut me down.

I try to form an identikit picture of it…

Its voice –
     would bellow

Feelings –
     a burning bruise

Colour –
     blackest of black

Age –
     Forever

Forever bellowing a big black bruise of despair.

I try to explain all this to my father, and as I do, his eyes focus on something behind me. It's like we're in combat, our own private war of me trying to get him to see inside me, and all the while he retreats to the safety of his dugout.

When my father enters my house, he can't help but see the massive display of photographs of you that cover the brick wall. He doesn't go in that room anymore. In fact, not many do now. In the afternoons, especially then for the sun hits the portrait and lights your eyes, I sit on the green velvet chair and study you. Try to imagine how you would look with a lined face, receding hair and gnarled hands. I can never age you.

'You've just got to get on with things,' says Dad.

'I do. I have. It's just that…'

'You're much too thin. How about a sandwich,' he says as more of a statement than a question. I watch this father of mine cut thick slabs of corned beef and squash them within slices of wholegrain bread.

'Have you gone back to your writing?' he says.

'Perhaps. When I thaw out.'

'You should. It'd do you good.'

He chews hard on his sandwich and I can feel his mind searching for something safe to talk about. Suddenly, it dawns on me that this man, my six foot father with his war medals, and a faded tattoo of a hawk on his arm, is afraid. For me?

'Though, I've started scribbling again. In dribs and drabs,' I say.

'I'm glad.'

'Do you want to hear some?'

I can tell he doesn't. Not safe enough. I take the journal from the top of the fridge and open it to yesterday's entry. 'It doesn't have a title.' And then, as soon as I say it, I wish I hadn't. 'I guess you could call it, "You just have to get on with things".'

His eyebrows meet as he frowns.

'It's a bit rough.'

'Yes,' he says, smarting from my snide remark, 'it was a bit rough.'

I take a deep breath, steel myself to read without a throat full of tears

Send out the posse
For she's lost her son
And grief nips at her heels
Boiling blisters that dry into scabs
Until the nipping grief erupts
Again and again

She sometimes sees him, her eldest
On a railway station
In a queue
Even in identikit pictures

She scans sunsets
Peers into mist
Keeps windows clean
She might miss him!

A lonely business this searching

It's like she's standing
On the stern of a ship
Stinging saltwater and westerly sun
A necessary punishment
As she scans the horizon
With binocular eyes
His bushy eyebrows stare back!
Oh…It's only arcing dolphins
Then the sun deceives

Living Death

The way it sears clouds into golden curls
Like when he was born

Waves tantalise her ankles
A conscious taste of oblivion
She could easily dive, fall
Into the blueness
That matches his eyes

But his eyes were brown!

See, that's why she must
Never stop searching
Must keep seeing his face
So she doesn't forget

She is the posse

When I have finished reading, my father looks at me, really looks at me, and says, 'I just wish…I wish I could buy a parcel of time for you. Three years' of time, and then you can bury it and so move on.'

I don't want time to evaporate. Every step forward is a memorial to you.

Chapter 17

Somehow I continue to surface when the alarm goes off, to serve decent meals at regular times, even to attack the weeds on a given day. Surface rhythms can be deceitful. But I must ape my previous existence, for on the other side of coping…well, best not think along those lines.

This day, instead of going to the cemetery to stand and stare at the parcel of land that conceals your bones, I go for a walk. The neighbourhood is quiet – no dogs, kids at school. The wind swirls the last of the recalcitrant autumn leaves. Aimlessly they fall. Loose skin from limbs shedding colours. I hold out my hands.

At home, in the study, I press the leaves between pages of the ponderous family Bible, and hope those pages are never again opened for the leaves will only disintegrate.

The carrots and potatoes are peeled, schnitzel crumbed, salad ready for tossing. I set the table for dinner. Nothing to fill the three hours till my family arrives home. I wander outside where the garden waits on the edge of spring. This early warmth has confused your tree for already it has blossomed. Soon the confettied branches will bow from the weight of apricots. I return to the study, scan the many books waiting to be read – *Tell Me I'm Here*, *Leaning Towards Infinity*, *Feeding the Demons*. I leave them waiting and go to the lounge, lie on the couch beneath your portrait and stare at you. I'd blow-waved your hair that day. Succeeded in getting the cow-lick to lay flat. Your trademark, I called it. An exclamation mark, you said. The sun lights up your eyes, traces your brow. Though your lips are closed to hide the shiny braces, as the sun lights your mouth you give me your crooked smile.

Eventually the sun finds me, and its warmth lulls me into a false sense of ease. Willingly I close my eyes and the nightmare that really happened, takes over…

You are dangling a line in the ocean. Suddenly, you're gone. All that remains on the wooden plank is your wallet and an empty beer can. You wander the city. No money for food. You sleep in an alleyway. When the night becomes grey, you go to Parliament Station for there's a chance she might catch the six o'clock rattler to work. Disheveled, you stand at the top of the underground escalators searching the mob as they ascend from the cavernous burrows. Your eyes search and search for your Goddess. A security guard tells you to move on. Loitering isn't allowed. You reach for your wallet to prove you're somebody. Frantically you search, but it's on the pier where you left it when your mates took you fishing with a slab of beer and a bag of bait. Even with a pole, tinny, and best friends you couldn't stop the pacing of your mind. One minute silhouetted by the moon, the next, an emptiness. A precursor of what was to come. The guard, menacing now, demands you move on. 'But I am somebody,' you say, 'I am. Ask my mother, she'll tell you.'

Another day I plan to go to the cemetery, instead find myself parked in the street where your Goddess lives. I don't remember driving here. In the warmth of the car I stare at the house with dilapidated shutters that seem to hang by threads. Over several hours I see the postman, the rubbish man, and children coming home from school. What had I expected to see? Your Goddess bent from grief, eyes raw from nightmares.

Another day I again plan to go to the cemetery, instead visit your Nan.

'Oh, everlasting daisies! Thanks,' she says, dropping them into a vase without water. That's probably where they'll stay until she's carted away. Usually she takes me to the back yard and I admire the fuchsias, geraniums and roses she's grown from cuttings. This time I won't go in the yard. We sit in the kitchen beside the wood stove where she cradled you in winter all those years ago. She talks about everything except you…the Liberal party, those bloody socialists who were ruining the country, and the pension.

'…I don't know how they expect us to live on such a measly amount. Why, bread and milk have gone up more than ten percent in the last months.' She stubs out a half-smoked cigarette, saving the rest for later.

Your photo sits on the bench, positioned so it faces your Nan's seat by the wood stove. For a while, we both stare at you.

'How are you coping with his death?' I ask.

She thinks for a moment. 'A bit easier. That photo you gave me. When I go to bed it's the last thing I see. The way you captured his expression. Head on an angle, cheeky grin, "Night Nan".'

Then she goes back to talking about safe things.

I have to use the toilet before I leave. Sitting on the stained bowl I tell myself I will not look out the narrow, cracked window to the corner of the yard. Will not look at the bottlebrush where you frantically tap-danced mid-air. When I do look, beneath the bottlebrush she's planted blue hyacinths. I like that. A bit like everlasting daisies really, hyacinths.

This day, I will definitely go to the cemetery. It's the morning of the thirteenth. I wake to a stillness, a holding breath sort of stillness, and not because for only the fifth time in thirty years there's to be a full moon on Friday thirteenth. More of a stillness because I have reached a grief stage where I've become a distillery of sorts. Simmering emotions waiting to be bottled.

I stand under a hot shower, timing how long I can hold my breath. How long does it take for lungs to run out of air? And does it happen quicker if you have a noose around your neck?

I've researched this hanging business. Know that the heart beats between eight and fifteen minutes after hanging. Strangulation occurs for a short drop; a broken neck for a long drop.

The doorbell rings as I'm drying myself, but I don't bother to answer it. Again it rings when I'm sitting at the table pulling the toast to bits.

A banging. It's FF at the kitchen window. 'Open the bloody door, would you!'

'Sorry,' I say, as I let her in.

'Didn't you hear the doorbell?'

'I couldn't be bothered.'

'Well, thanks very much!'

'I didn't know it was you.'

She sits beside me, clutching a parcel. Pushes the hair off my face. 'You shouldn't sit around with wet hair. You'll catch a cold.'

'I'll drop it then!'

She smiles, shakes her head. 'What am I going to do with you?'

'More, what am I going to do with myself?'

'Here, this is for you.'

She busies herself clearing the table, while I unwrap the floral material that protects a wooden sculpture. It appears androgynous, no breasts, no face. But I know it represents a woman by the tilt of the head, the empty arms, one foot slightly exposed, toes peeping from beneath a robe. Grief and vulnerability.

'You make this?'

'Just another one of my claims to fame,' she says.

'It's beautiful.'

'I've called it 'After the Pieta.''

'Sounds like a pizza,' I say, in an effort to mask how deeply the statue affects me.

'It's religious, you atheist. The Pieta was when Jesus was taken from the cross and put in his mother's arms.'

'But her arms are empty,' I say, referring to the sculpture.

'It's after the Pieta.'

Suddenly I understand. And it doesn't matter I'm an atheist, Mary's grief is mine. I take the statue into the lounge and place it on the glass table where the sun shines most.

Later, we make the pilgrimage together, FF and me. Someone else has recently been to see you, for there's a half-smoked reefer, and a near-empty can of beer beside your plaque.

We stand there, looking down on the words:

> Adored son, brother, grandson
> Your love lights our way
> Your memory forever with us

'Original,' I say.

'Spot on,' says FF.

From my pocket I take handfuls of blood-red petals, and scatter them over you.

'These are from his rosebush,' I tell FF. 'The one I bought especially.' It grows outside my bedroom window and on a still night I lie in bed and breathe in the fragrance of you. I don't tell FF that the rosebush was second choice. I'd wanted a rambling rose, for that's how I thought of you. A tall rambler who occasionally bloomed, and when you did your scent permeated everything. At the nursery, my husband following close behind, I'd marched up and down the aisles as if on a mission. Finally, in the far corner, I found what I'd been looking for. Pots and pots of rambling roses. I chose a blood-red climber. My husband said we had no room for it. By the pool, I said, just near the grape vine. He told me, No, that he was the one who cleaned the pool and it got enough shit in it already.

'Second-best is better than nothing,' I say, reflecting on that day at the nursery.

'First-rate', says FF, misinterpreting me. She places a gladiolus on your grave. A gladiolus she's stolen from the grave beside you. 'He was first-rate.'

Just five days later, I stand outside the weatherboard house, paint peeling like sunburn, weeds choking what's left of the garden. On the narrow verandah is a couch, brown vinyl and ripped, and a spew-orange chair that sags in the middle like a prolapsed womb. The sort of house you normally see set back from the highway, remote and sad. I've often wondered when passing these homes, why they have their lounge on the verandah. Do they have so much time on their hands they can sit and watch people pass by? Or, perhaps it's a silent invitation for people to stop and sit awhile.

I know she's not home, your Goddess. I waited and watched at the end of the street until she reversed the old Holden out of the driveway. She has blonde hair now, down to her shoulders. When you brought her over for us to meet that one time, her hair was a purple cocky's crest. My lasting memory of that day is how, after we'd eaten under the grape vine, you both went to the farthest end of the pool and sat on the edge, dangling legs in the water. Watching you both muttering away, I felt liberated. For the first time in twenty-nine years you had a woman, other than me, to share your thoughts.

Boldly I walk up the driveway and around the back. In the far corner of the yard is an outside dunny, and beside that, a large kennel, the word 'Cujo' crudely painted red on the roof. I stand very still. Sneak a hand into my robbery bag, a plastic bag with 'just in case' odds and ends. Though I don't intend to steal anything. I just want to see if there're any bits of you left here. I whistle, wave the chop in the air, call, 'Cujo. Here boy.'

You had a dog. It sits uneasy with me that time. Doing the right thing, then the wrong thing. When your brother was born you were ten. I thought a dog would give you a focus away from what you might perceive as my sudden lack of attention.

'Just don't get a dog that's too big, will you,' I said, the morning you were off to choose one from the Lost Dog's Home. 'Are you both listening to me?'

'Just this big,' you said, measuring the air with your hand.

'That's too big!'

'We've got plenty of room for it to run,' said my husband.

'Well, small to medium then,' I said, as I waved you both off.

When you returned with Rascal, who was large to extra large, I gave my husband one of my 'See what you've gone and done' looks. The shrug of his shoulders said, 'What could I do?'

'He looked so sad, Mum.'

'Well, he certainly looks happy now.'

We watched as you ran around the backyard. Laughed as you tried to teach him to sit.

'That dog is going to be too big,' I told my husband.

'Your son is stubborn like you. No way could I dissuade him.'

When your brother woke, you insisted on a formal meeting. First taking the cot blanket for Rascal to smell, then bringing your brother to be smelt. The longest tongue licked your brother's face, the biggest paw tap, tapped his tiny chest.

'That's enough now. Take him outside. Give him some water.'

'But he only wants to play.'

'Go on. Out!'

If you weren't hovering over the cot, watching your brother breathe, you were out in the yard throwing a frisbee for Rascal. Everyone who came to see our new baby, you'd take outside to meet your dog.

As your brother grew, so did Rascal, paws the size of my palm.

One sunny day, I put your brother in the pram and parked him outside to catch the warmth. A fitted, green mosquito net covers the pram. Rascal circles the pram, sniffing. The phone rings. I rush inside to answer. From the window I watch the pram and the dog. The doorbell rings, so I ask the caller to hang on, and rush to the front door. Avon calling. I get rid of her quickly. As I pick up the phone I look out the window.

The mosquito net is ripped. The dog taps my baby's head. I jump the last six steps of the spiral staircase. No sound, not even a growl from the dog, or a whimper from the pram. The dog salivates, and now his huge paws dig at the blanket that covers my son. The dog seems the weight of a Shetland pony, but somehow I manage to pull him away. I hold my baby so very tight as I run upstairs. The dog whimpers at the closed door. I sit at the table, soothing my son, all the while staring at the brown door as if waiting for a snake to squeeze beneath.

'But Rascal wouldn't hurt him, Mum. He wouldn't. I know he wouldn't,' you said, when you returned from school and I told you what happened.

That night, as we sat eating our meal, your brother asleep in the cot, just the one deep scratch on his cheek, I again told you how afraid I was that the dog would hurt your brother. Again, you insisted Rascal was just playing, he wouldn't mean to hurt anyone.

'But you see, I can't trust him near the baby. He might hurt him.'

You toyed with the peas and corn, then said, 'Does that mean I have to take him back?'

'No. You don't have to. It's your decision. But would you feel safe leaving Rascal alone with your brother?'

I should have made the decision for you, coward that I am.

The next morning you spent time outside playing with Rascal, and then told me that you'd take him back to the Dogs' Home.

We never did get you a replacement dog.

Again I whistle, wave the chop in the air. Cujo must not exist. I put the meat back in the bag. The back door is wooden, round handle rusted. I was hoping it wouldn't be locked. My parents never locked their back door, didn't even have a key. When they went on their annual camping trip, Dad hammered six nails in the door. No matter, I have come prepared. I slide the file between the door and the jamb.

Inside, a dog lies on the cracked lino, head resting on its paws, eyelids slowly blinking over filmy eyes. 'Here, Cujo.' I offer the chop. He sniffs the air. I move closer, one slow step at a time. He must be blind for he doesn't react until the chop touches his nose. Old too, for his teeth are putrid. I leave him to gorge on my bribe.

Faded carpet leads me up the hallway to the lounge. Two brown vinyl chairs that match the couch on the verandah huddle around a gas fire. There's a bong on the floor. Beneath the window, a potted plant stretches towards the slanting sun. I stand in this room, where you once sat, look at the television you once watched. Did you make one of the stains on the carpet? There's a print of McCubbin's. I stare at the picture of morning dew veiling gum trees. Incongruous against nicotine-stained walls. You would have stared at the print, imagined yourself in that scene. Eyes closed, I stand in the centre of the room and try to breathe your smell. Nothing.

I continue up the faded carpet to the end room. Slowly, ever so slowly, I open the door and as I do, I realise how foolish I've been. Just because she's left the house, doesn't necessarily mean it's empty of people. The bed is unmade, daisy patterned pillow-cases and the whitest sheets. This is the bed you sometimes slept in. Near the window is a hat stand where Op-shop looking hats hang, as if waiting for an invitation. Two photos are displayed on the bedside table; one of a newborn baby, a name tag still on its wrist. Your Goddess is in the other photo, wearing the purple hat from the stand. She holds an older baby rigged out in what looks like a christening dress. She must be the Godmother.

I see three of me in the mirror that has a middle and two sides. The dressing table is antique, the sort my grandfather left me in his will. I open a drawer and search through the g-strings and Tampax boxes.

I find your image in the left hand drawer beneath tangled jewellery. I haven't seen this photo of you. It's been ripped in half, then sticky-taped back together. Your head is thrown back, mouth wide open, crinkled eyes. I don't remember seeing you laugh like this. So freed up.

A car door slams. I go to the window, peer through the scrim.

Only Mrs Next Door. What if your Goddess hasn't gone to work, is just out on a message? I put your photo in the drawer. Then in my pocket. She doesn't deserve you.

On my way out, I pass two closed doors. No time to look inside. Next time. But there won't be a next time for I have taken the only thing of value.

Driving home I feel no guilt for I had every right to be there. Every right to go where you have been. As I round the corner to my street, I recognise the red sports car parked outside my home. Reclined in the seat, FF waves as I approach.

'I've been waiting for ages! Where've you been?'

'Why?'

'Because I'm taking you to lunch. Did you forget?'

'Just got held up.' The thing was, I had forgotten. I was forgetting lots lately.

'Well powder your nose, girl, and get out of that daggy tracksuit. I'll give you five minutes.'

FF powers up the freeway, the car hood still down, music blaring. My hair comes loose and streams behind me.

'We must look like Thelma and Louise,' shouts FF.

'We are Thelma and Louise!'

'Well, thank God there are no cliffs around here!'

'We could find one easily enough,' I say.

She gives me one of her looks. 'Where were you this morning?'

I save myself from lying by singing along with the deep voice coming from the radio...lyrics that plead to walk with you and talk to you what's in my soul.

'Where exactly are we going?' I ask.

'Yarra Valley. Thought we'd lunch at a winery. But before that, I want to deliver an order to a dear friend. He's getting a bit toey. Should have delivered it last week. It's an anniversary present for his wife.'

I'm fiddling with the radio, trying to find a song that doesn't remind me of you, when FF says, 'You know, I'm really worried about you.'

'Why's that?'

'You're not yourself. It's like…oh forget it, I'm just being selfish.'

'No. Go on!'

'It's just that…I want the old you back.'

'Me too. But there's no hope of that.'

'Course there is.'

'You know, I can't even remember what she was like anymore.'

'She was funny. Crazy-funny. She had me wetting my pants more than I ever will from incontinence. But now she's…'

I turn up the volume. Someone's singing about the dead who dance. I study the dashed line in the middle of the road.

The right-hand indicator flashes, and we overtake a station wagon filled with a family going somewhere. The wind blows her words, but I think she says, 'Sorrow has become your nourishment.' Yes, I'm sure that's what she said.

We turn into a driveway lined with huge, bare trees, and pull up outside a mud-brick house, dogs barking our arrival. A woman with white hair and weathered skin comes to the door, peers out. 'I'll keep her busy,' says FF, 'while you stash the loot in the shed over there.'

The huge shed is hot, airless, and full of colour. It's like I've walked into a craft shop. Statuettes, plates, bowls, goblets and mugs decorate the many shelves.

'Hi there!' says a deep voice.

In the far corner, by the window, a man, legs spread, sits shaping clay.

'Feel free to look around.'

'I come bearing a gift.' I hold out the gift as if proof is needed.

'Ah, the anniversary present. She made the deadline, after all.' He nods towards a large glazed urn. 'Hide it in there. My wife never dusts, so there's no chance of her finding it.'

'So, you're a potter, then,' I say, stating the obvious.

He shrugs. Starts the wheel turning. 'Try to be.'

'Is it a difficult process?' I ask, not really caring one way or the other.

'The main thing you need to remember,' he says, his focus on shaping whatever he's creating, 'is clay has feelings. Clay remembers. That's why it can crack when you fire it. So, as you mould the bowl you must apply enormous pressure, over and over to make the clay forget.'

Even if I'm to crack, no hands will make me forget.

'Forget what?' he asks, and I realise I'm speaking my thoughts.

And now all this time later, there are days I wonder if what follows really happened. Or, needing a way of tacking my ripped heart, I imagined it all. No matter, it gave me the chance to bond one last time with my beautiful son.

Chapter 18

I would never have gone back if I hadn't read the letters you wrote your Goddess; the ones the coroner sent me, the ones I'd sealed in the file marked with your name. Sealed until I had some distance from your death. Last night I opened the letters for I now know there never will be distance from your death.

I stand in the drizzling rain, watching and waiting. The letters are zipped into the side pocket of the bag that digs into my shoulder like an angry reminder. Even with my eyes closed, I still see the cursive letters making your words of entreaty.

It's not only the letters that have bought me here on this dismal Tuesday morning. I also unsealed the statement she made to the police. She said you phoned her just after eleven on the night you died. So it was immediately after that call you sat on the bed and ripped your trackie pants into strips, making a plaited noose.

Across the road a woman manoeuvres a shopping jeep through a gate. She closes the gate behind her, checks the latch is in place, looks to the sky, unfolds a plastic rain hat, the concertinaed sort, and fastens it with a bow under her chin.

She notices me. I bend, pretend to fasten the clasp on my shoe. Still she stares. I feel her eyes sussing me out as I briskly walk away.

Some time later – ten? twenty? thirty minutes? I stand on your Goddess' porch. I don't remember where I've walked. The rain has stopped and the sun steams the wet path. I draw back the lion's head doorknocker and let it fall. Again and again I pull back the lion's head. Bang! Bang! Each bang shakes the leadlight window set in the door. Ruby triangles to make everything look rosy.

Behind the leadlight, a shadow hovers. I move so the shadow sees mine. The door opens. We stand there as if trying to outstare each other. When she recognises me there is just the slightest widening of eyes. She looks different, younger, her face free of the heavy makeup she wore that time I met her. Your death hasn't eaten away at her, for she's put on weight.

'Yes,' she says. Then, 'Yes!'

'I need to speak with you.'

'What about?'

'My son.'

'Look, I don't…'

I put my foot on the doorstep. 'It won't take a moment.' She stands aside and I resist the urge to turn and run, to leave buried what I must dig.

I follow her to the lounge where the old dog lies by the heater. She closes the sliding glass doors, sits in the brown, vinyl chair, doesn't offer me a seat.

'What is it you want?'

I take the letters from the bag and hand them to her. She opens one, then the other, not even a tremble as she holds your words.

'What are you doing with these? They're mine!'

I say nothing, in the hope silence will unnerve her. Ill-at-ease people often talk themselves into a corner. She puts the letters on the coffee table. I see the upside down words…

All my love…Soulmate…Forever yours

'Look, what d'ya want from me?'

'I've just a few questions. I need to understand…'

She raises an eyebrow, the one pierced with a gold ring. 'Sometimes there are no answers.' The dog leaves the fire and stands at the glass doors. She looks at the wall clock. I take your last letter, begin to read aloud…

> Why do you refuse to have anything to do with me again? I can truly accept this if you tell me why. An honest answer will help me move on. Such love we shared. Whoever next takes your heart, I hope he's honest and respectful towards you.

> PS If you ever need a friend you know where I am (at the moment?)
> My love, forever.

The dog whines. Again she looks at the clock.

In the silence I say, 'Didn't you think it an odd thing to write…"You know where I am…at the moment"?'

She shrugs. 'I told the cops just that when I did the statement.' She stands. 'Is that all?'

I won't be put off. The dog can wait for its walk.

'In your statement you say my son phoned you just after eleven the night he died.'

'So?'

'I spoke with him minutes before then. He seemed settled. I was going to pick him up in the morning. He was looking forward to spending a day with me. We had all sorts of things planned…'

The dog scratches at the door. She goes to open it, but I stand in front, blocking the way. She shoves me aside. The dog follows her up the hallway, and I'm left with just your upside down words…

> …lovely and special as you…I wish I lived up to your expectations…A girl I will hold close to my heart forever.

Her shadow passes the frosted glass where a peacock is etched on the doors. Eventually there's the zing of a microwave and she returns with a baby swaddled in a blue blanket. Greedily it sucks at the bottle. The dog settles at her feet.

'What did you say to my son?'

'When?'

'That last conversation.'

'Nothin' that I hadn't said before.'

I lean forward. 'Please, I need to know.'

The baby cries; she puts it on her shoulder, rubs its back in a circular motion.

'He wished me all the happiness in the world. That's why he rang.' She stares me down.

'And you. What did you say?'

'Just this and that. Can't remember, really.'

'Oh really! Yet you can recall his words.'

The baby screams. She unwraps the blanket, lays the baby over her knees, continues rubbing its back, says, 'Mummy will make it better.'

I concentrate hard, refusing to let a mop of blonde hair with a cowlick distract me.

'I know he found out that very day that you had another boyfriend. One you'd had for a few months. Did he ask you about that?'

She nestles the baby in her arms, and it again begins sucking at the bottle. 'Can't remember.'

'Well, I can! In our last conversation he told me he'd just found out all along you had another boyfriend. 'It cuts so deep', he said, 'It cuts so deep, Mum. Why didn't she tell me? I thought it was me, that something was wrong with me.' It was your deceit that crippled him. How long had you been deceiving my son? Answer me!'

Just the sound of sucking air. She puts the empty bottle on the table, wraps the blanket around the sleepy baby.

'Why weren't you honest with him?'

'Sometimes honesty hurts too much.' She stands. 'Look you'd better go.'

'He loved you, really loved you. Christ, just weeks before he died, you were choosing furniture with him, planning to set up home together! And you had your new love going at the same time!'

'I wish things could've been different. I really do.'

The baby peers from within the folds of the blanket. She pulls the blanket so its face is hidden from me.

'Do you make a practice of leaving dead boyfriends behind you?'

This stops her short. She holds the baby too tight, for it wriggles to escape her clutches.

'In your statement, you say you met my son just a week before your boyfriend killed himself.'

'That's got nothin' to do with you.'

I stand close to her, so close I can taste the ugly smell of her mouth. 'It's got everything to do with me. Anything to do with my son has everything to do with me!'

'That's an invasion of privacy! You shouldn't have my statement.'

'An invasion of privacy! You invaded my son's life!' I'm screaming, but I don't care that the dog whines and the baby cries. 'You fucking invaded and raided and decimated my son's life. And you can stand there and whinge about an invasion of privacy!'

'If you don't go, I'll call the police.' She backs up to the chair.

'Odd, isn't it, that two men you've had a relationship with have killed themselves.'

'So? These things happen. Don't point the finger at me. It was your son who was weak. He had the mental condition, not me!'

I go to slap her face. She raises an arm to lash out, but I'm stronger than her. Arm-wrestling mid-air.

'Get out,' she hisses. She tilts to the side and without taking her eyes off me, picks up the bong from beside the chair and waves it near my face. 'Get out and don't ever come back. If you do, I'll call the police.' I walk backwards down the hallway. She follows, the glass bong raised, ready to smash my head.

I sit in my car, unable to drive. So afraid of these unfamiliar feelings that make me tremble like a willow in the wind. You can dislike people, my father once told me, but don't ever hate. Hate is a vicious emotion that can go nowhere. Well, sorry to disappoint you, Dad…hatred consumes me; Dad, hatred consumes me.

After you died, FF said you can tell the depth of a person by the emptiness they leave behind. The gap that is your absence is so vast many worlds could fit within. And look at her! If she felt your absence, she more than filled the gap with her lover. And now a baby.

Over the next weeks I try to do the usual, but I'm only half there, stop-starting too many jobs at the one time, never getting anywhere but muddled. The baby's face keeps intruding. Stares at me from within the blue blanket. Pointed chin, big ears, and a cowlick like an exclamation mark.

The baby has blue eyes. Yours are brown. But then most babies have blue eyes, especially those with blonde hair. In the beginning, you had blonde hair.

I wonder how old the baby is. I make myself stop wondering by attacking half-finished projects like cleaning the front windows, planting the last of the pansies under the weeping cherry. And as I plant them two inches apart, the words in her statement rebound:

Just a few weeks before he died, I'd met another man I loved and so decided to break up with him for good. When I told him that, I told him in person and he seemed to take it okay and didn't appear very sad, although I remember he seemed a little shocked.

Liar, liar, pants on fire! My son never knew of the other man.

My son told me this just an hour before he killed himself. Bitch!
You cuckolded my son.

The line of seedlings is skewed. I uproot them. It's while I'm concentrating on replanting the pansies, rotating the colours of
purple and yellow, that the face of her baby appears. And no
matter how much I shake my head in an effort to dislodge the
vision, his face closes in on me. He looks to be about ten months.
So that means, he could be... And that cowlick!

Chapter 19

He is in the pram on the porch. Little hands and feet punch holes in the air, like he is trying to box his way out. He knows I'm here, watching over him.

I imagine insects flitting and darting, and I'm cross she hasn't a net over the pram. Never, ever did I leave you outside without a fitted net. I imagine a bee settles on his nose, attracted by his sweet innocence.

Gurgles turn to grizzles. Where is she? She doesn't care. The pram rocks from his agitated soul.

I step over the rusty gate for I remember from my last visit how it squeaks when opened. Thirteen steps. My lucky number.

I only wanted to look at him, but when I hold him close, snuggle my face into his creased neck, smell the scent of innocence; I feel my heart beating for the first time since you left me.

I mustn't run. Mustn't risk falling and damaging you. You watch the shadows we leave behind.

In the car, I sit you on my lap, and secure us together with the seat belt. Your belly touches the steering wheel. As we drive past the house, she still hasn't come to check on you. She doesn't deserve you.

I am thirsty. How long have I been driving? Asleep now, your head falls onto the wheel. With my left hand, I hold you upright. My lap is wet from you. I drive in a straight line, for I can't turn the wheel with one hand.

The sun shines everywhere. And everywhere is where you are. With me. My thirst is such that I feel it will never be quenched. I turn into a Safeway, find a shady spot to park. Mustn't overheat you.

You fit snug on my hip as I hurry up and down the aisles, grabbing bottled water, plastic training cup, dummy, milk and bananas. Just as I am about to leave, I remember how much you love Marie biscuits, the ones the baby health centre sister recommended. I buy two packets. As I am about to check out under the sign, '12 Items or Less', I remember the treacle.

We drive on, strapped together. You stare out the window like a Learner driver out of his depth.

In the park, I lay you on the picnic blanket I carry in the boot. You roll over. 'Mum,mum,mum,mum,' you say, and I know you are asking for a drink.

'See, you don't need a bottle. You're a big boy now. You can drink from a cup.' So greedily you suck on the spout. Milk dribbles from the corner of your mouth.

I lay you on the blanket, and unclip the jumpsuit that's wet through. Oh, dear, I forgot to put a singlet on you this morning. What a duffer! Oh, well, the sun will keep you warm. I take off your nappy. Pump your plump legs so the air circulates around your bottom. We don't want a rash. The jumpsuit I spread on a low hanging branch. I lie down beside you. You poke a finger in my eye. And then you grab at my nose. You smile – just the one lonely tooth.

I grab you to me, roll on my back, and lay you on my stomach. Our hearts pump together. We mirror each other. I feel the tug of the umbilical cord. Unbroken.

'Oh, you are such a good boy!' Look at how you lie there, not crying, just checking everything out with big round eyes that miss nothing. You stare into mine. I take your hand, trace circles in the palm, sing:

Living Death

Round and round the garden
Like a teddy bear
One step, two step,
Tickle me under there

Oh, so long since I've heard your laugh. A laugh is like a thumbprint. Yours has a squeal that ends in a giggle. Then you get a fit of the giggles. I do the same to your other hand.

I take you bare foot, plant raspberry kisses on the heel. Your special laugh again. The other foot now. Then I raspberry kiss your midriff, turn you over and raspberry kiss your bum. Such squeals! A dog comes bounding to inspect what's happening, followed by its owner.

'What fun you're having!' says the woman, holding a leash. 'How old is he?'

'As old as I want him to be.'

She smiles as though she understands, clips the dog onto the leash, and leaves us.

Lying with you, skin to skin, I will never want for anything. Warmth trickles over my midriff, and then it's my turn to get the giggles as your little spout sporadically spurts urine. My miniature fireman.

Suddenly, we are stripped of the sun's blanket. You shudder, and begin to cry. The jumpsuit is nearly dry. I fashion a nappy out of my spencer. You cry even more as I push your little limbs into the arms and legs of the blue jumpsuit. I wrap you in the blanket. Hungry, you must be hungry. I nearly forget and swallow the banana I masticate for you. You've always loved bananas. An egg and a banana – the staple diet for eating out! As quickly as I chew, you swallow what I've offered. I peel another banana, but you eat only half. The milk smells all right, but I can't be sure. You spit out the water I offer.

Still clouds hide the sun. I gather you to me and run for the car, just in time to escape the pelting rain. And there we sit, just you and me, watching raindrops race themselves down the windows. I dip the dummy in treacle and stick it to your eyelid. Quickly I lick the treacle from your eyelid for I'm reminded of that frozen death wink. Was it yesterday, or decades, ago, when in the dark, I dipped the dummy in treacle and, without getting out of bed, reached over and popped the dummy in your mouth? You stopped crying. And when it was light, you were lying there waiting for me to take the dummy that was stuck to your eyelid. Remember how I then too, licked the treacle from your skin. You my fledgling, me your mother, the one who thought she could always protect you.

It is dark now. Cold. I turn the ignition. Start the heater. So very dark. The windscreen wipers mesmerise. We are bound together. And here we shall stay, cocooned from the world.

Cocooned from the world, but not my thoughts

All night I think on our long journey. Stare at how peacefully you sleep in my arms. So much anguish has gone before. Layer upon layer of burning anguish. I think of your Goddess. How she is now about to walk the Anguish Path that leads to Nowhere. She would not be able to bear it.

When the stars fade, and dawn silhouettes the swings and roundabout, I know what I must do. You are not mine to keep. You were only on loan, but nobody bothered to tell me.

Acknowledgements

--

This story would not be complete without acknowledging my Writerly Friends who during my deepest grief, threw me a lifeline with words. Six months after my son's death, they insisted our work-shopping continue, and so on a regular Saturday we'd meet at a Carlton café to share our work. No longer did I have reams of words for them; it was difficult enough just breathing…instead just a few lines, a verse, was all I could manage. They listened and nodded and rubbed my back as I mourned my son with written emotions. That collection of poems became the spring-board for the prose.

You wonderful women

Jenny Mooney
Jan Stumbles
Gabrielle Daly

My Writerly Friends, and oh, so much more!

About Janis Tait

Janis Tait is mother to three and friend to many. She has been writing for fifteen years, been published in literary magazines and won National Short Story Awards. She also works in the Aged Care Industry and is a Civil Celebrant. Janis lives with her husband in Melbourne, Australia.

Janis can be contacted on www.janistait.com

Written feelings to my son

Surprise!

I hate being surprised

Most surprises are awful
Like parties
When everyone yells SURPRISE!
And you're standing there
With wax on your lips

**Shocked stillness
of
Autumn**

There's other sorts, like
CONGRATULATIONS, You're
pregnant!
And you smile while you decide
How to get a day off work
To stop anyone else being
surprised

Or

You take Grandma a bunch of
roses
Only to find her stiff beneath the
clothesline

The only sort of surprises I like
are
When you go to empty the
dishwasher
And it's been done

The worst, the very worst
surprise is
The 'phone screeching in the
middle of the night
And you're left open-mouthed
Forever

May 2000

It should have rained!

In the movies it rains at funerals
Umbrellas and dark coats
To match the cloud of fear
That it could be theirs next time

It should have rained
Yet the sun shone
Dissolving their fear
As if a figment of imagination

You were not a figment
But a filigree
Fragile, transparent
Yet…
So whole

May 2000

Weightless

The deepest well of tears

Useless to try to bucket them
Floods of tears won't change
anything
Dead is dead
Even if there is an after-life
It's out of huggable reach

I nearly sink
From the weight of these tears
That can't be measured
Like a barrel of beer or a case
of spuds
Limitless they are

In my youth
I was once heartbroken
Afraid my heavy heart
Would 'plop' onto the floor
Everyone seeing my despair

It's different this time for
Weight pervades every sinew
Impossible to grasp, dislodge

Yesterday I spent hours digging
At the stubborn root of a cherry
blossom
It would have taken you
5 minutes
This is just one of the ways
I miss you

May 2000

Rejoice

She has so much to rejoice over
What they mean is
I don't know how to make
it better

So when I think on you
I rejoice that I knew you
That you knew me

But did we really know each
other?

May 2000

Look Back But Don't Stare

How can I not?
How can I not reach for
Those untouchable feelings
Our arms can no longer embrace
Not ever

Frozen state
of
Winter

Things like
Your crooked smile
Brown eyes
And those perfect sausage rolls
you made

Only if I stare can I truly feel

June 2000

The Therapist

She sits there listening
Mouth agape
Silent scissors
Fixed eyes
As she hears what I have to say
Of how
The noose was his trackie pants
Swollen tongue; Pacific blue

When I'm finished staring back
She sighs
Holds a mirror behind my head
So I can still see backwards

June 2000

Air

When the sun's behind me
My shadow covers the rectangle
That was a clay mound
And is now carpeted with lawn
Keeping you warm

Some say I must feel angry at
you
How can I?
When every time I breathe it
hurts
A wide hole that
Lets in the moaning wind
To rattle my senses

If you hurt like this
Every time you took a breath
Then how can I be angry
That you decided to stop
breathing

June 2000

Clouds

If you lose things like…

A purse
You become broke

Virginity
You become a woman

A husband
You become a widow

A last parent
You become an orphan

What do you become
When you lose a son?

Sunless

June 2000

Last Dance

Lament the Lamented
Is not a dance like
Begin the Beguine

There is no dance of death
Just a shuffle, shuffle into the
night
That has no dawn

June 2000

Those Words

She stands in front of the mirror
Practicing
Practicing the words
That usually flow
So matter-of-fact
Words…as if just placing a
grocery order

Now…
Force a tear, a sob
Try to make the words
Catch on barbed wire

My son died last year

See, simple as adding
String beans to the shopping list

Still she practices for
She's never bought string beans

June 2000

Feelings

I feel guilty…

When I find myself
Head thrown back
As if to catch the breeze from my
laughter

Or…

When I look in the mirror and
Like what I see
If I go 4 hours without thinking
on you
For not having taken enough
photos

Even guiltier
That I only gave you $20 that
time

And for silly things like
Plucking my eyebrows
(as if they matter in the scheme
of things)

Still, I refuse to stop feeling
For while I do
You'll stay with me

June 2000

The Message

That night
When the crescent moon
Hung crooked in sorrow
I read the pamphlet from the
Coroner
Instructions on coping and
autopsy rituals

You came to me then
Sprinkling glitter on the oak table
Over tracks in the dust my
fingers had made
As I registered the need to clean
before the wake

Glitter…
So unlike you

But then…
Hanging was most unlike you,
too

June 2000

Clay

You must remember, he says
Clay has feelings

His hands cup an imaginary
bowl
Clay remembers
That's why it cracks when you
fire it

As you mould the bowl
You must apply enormous
pressure
Over and over
To make the clay forget

Even if I'm to crack
No hands will make me forget

July 2000

Imagery

On the edge of sleep
Sharp intakes of breath
As imagery invades the stillness

Chipped ashtray; wiped clean
Empty brandy bottle; in the bin
Wallet; on the kitchen table
The note beneath

So sorry, so very, very sorry.

Bottlebrush in the corner
Branches bent from your weight
Brick edging skewed from final
mid-air steps
Blue tongue
Yellow sun rising

July 2000

Generation Gaps

In photos I confuse you with
your brother
It scares me
That likeness
Appearances can be deceptive
But I must not deceive myself
It can happen to any one of us

And it did
Though skipping a generation

Grandfather;
All those years in that chair
Just a pipe and jam tin for a
spittoon

Nephew;
Departed on a heroin track

Niece;
Her head in the oven.
Underdone

Cousin;
On a mountain
Lost in the clouds

Yet another;
Being saved in the nick of time
As he more than nicks himself

Living Death

And there's my son
And there's me on Prozac

While outside my bedroom
window
An azalea withers
Though not from disease, purely
lack of water
Or so the nurseryman tells me

July 2000

Seasonal

When he was first dead, she said

First dead?

Are there parts to death
Like seasons?

First dead;
A frozen Wintry state

Recently dead;
The shocked stillness of Autumn

Died some time ago;
Spring growth emerging from
the bone compost

A long time dead;
Sultry steaming Summer
sweating tears

July 2000

Cadaver

Stooping to collect Mother of
Pearl shells
That smell of salt and time

Stooping to lay baby tears
On the rectangle of lawn

Though you're a buried shell
I still smell you

July 2000

Will-O-Wisp

I got your note the other night
Didn't open it
Not at first
I knew what it said
Though I did open a corner
Just to make sure
And recognised the adderly
stroke of your Sssss

So sorry, so very, very sorry.

As always now
Before going to bed
I went outside
And while the cats dug in
the soil
I stood before your apricot tree

Now that Winter nears its' end
Blossoms scatter your tree
Like will-o-wisps caught
mid-flight
And I remembered that day

You'd just arrived home
Overwrought
Vowing never to return to that
place
Not ever
No matter what

Though the sun shone you
were cold
Fingers poking through
woollen gloves
I'd bought to warm you
in that place
I watched my strapping
six foot son
Wearing an Essendon beanie
Watched how you weeded a
space around a thistle
Insisting it was a marijuana plant

Suddenly your gaze was on the
peach and plum trees
Why didn't I get one, too?
But you were 17 when I planted
the garden
Your brothers little boys
I just didn't think…

I took your poking fingers
Led you to the nursery

How you deliberated!
Rejecting this one
For its branches were out
of shape
That one
For it was too short
Then…
This one 'because it just feels
right'

We became like anxious parents,
You and I
Waiting 5 years for your tree to
flower
Last Spring the blossoms were
many

The fruit ripened as you rotted in
the ground

When the house was quiet
And the cats settled for the night
I held the envelope that hid your
note

I had to have that note
The original

So sorry, so very, very sorry

Your last words?
Or did you curse as you tried
To fasten the noose around the
bottlebrush
(at least you didn't choose a
fruit tree!)

I threw out the envelope marked
"State Coroner's Office"
And the letter that said
As requested, find attached the
original note left by your son

197

Your final words now rest in the
old writing case
Alongside the final note
Your great-grandmother wrote to
my father

When Summer arrives I shall
pick your peaches
Hoard them as I did last year
And this starved woman
Shall again eat the apricots that
are the
Flesh of my son
Juice of my tears

So sorry, so very, very sorry.

August 2000

Pummeling

The flailing fist inside my chest
Is just one of the ways my pain
escapes

If, momentarily, the flailing stops
The pulsing pain of bitten down
quicks
Remind me

August 2000

The Missing Bit

If I had aborted you
What would you have missed?

Not hitting a six or making a
century
Pushing your brothers in that
billycart you made
Flying high on that stuff you
liked to smoke
Demons who set up camp in
your head
Loyalty of a mate who followed
you to the end and beyond
Fishing off rocks at Wye River
Legs entwined in your lovers'
Essendon winning a premiership
The taste of beer and love
Smell of seasons and manure
A steel rod in your leg
A dutiful father
Disappointment, frustration,
alcoholism
A step-father who tried so hard,
but still it came out wrong
A grandfather who couldn't
understand
Uncles who got you plastered
when you turned 18
Hitting the jackpot at the pokies
Cleaning my stove
Giggling with your brothers
Making the best sausage rolls

Nearly drowning in the spa at
your 21st

But most of all…
You would have missed me

August 2000

The Posse

Send out the posse
For she's lost her son
And grief nips at her heels

Boiling blisters that dry into
scabs
Until the nipping grief erupts
Again and again

She sometimes see him, her
eldest
On a railway station
In a queue
Even in identikit pictures

She scans sunsets
Peers into mist
Keeps windows clean
She might miss him!

A lonely business this searching

It's like she's standing
On the stern of a ship
Stinging saltwater and westerly
sun
A necessary punishment
As she scans the horizon
With binocular eyes

His bushy eyebrows stare back!
It's only arcing dolphins
Then the sun deceives
The way it sears a cloud into
golden curls
Like when he was born

Waves tantalise her ankles
A conscious taste of oblivion
She could easily dive, fall into
the blueness
That matches his eyes

But his eyes were brown!

See, that's why she must never
stop searching
Must keep seeing his face
So she doesn't forget

She is the posse

August 2000

King Tide

He's stopping mentioning you
Is unable to reach me in my
distress
Afraid
Afraid if he does it might ignite
Feelings, questions, answers
even
That he prefers to stay buried
Safer not to scratch at the scabs
For if you scratch too deep
An artery might burst
And he's got no means
To still a river of blood

Marooned I remain
Not even dashes or dots
Can alert him to my distress

And so I sit on my island
Waiting for a King Tide
To carry me to that place that
must exist
A place where I'll be weightless
From the joy of sharing sorrow

August 2000

Becalmed

When I am becalmed by that
stillness
I sift through your still life
Wishing you were smiling in
this one
Or that your eyes weren't red
from the flash
Annoyed that you were so
camera shy

When I find what fits
The stillness goes
Replaced by anxiety as I tell the
girl
How big I want it and
'I won't lose any definition,
will I?' and
'Show me exactly what size he'll
be then'

I hang your photo
Stand back
Aware how each time the
stillness takes hold
Your photo's bigger than the last

August 2000

This place

In this damp place
A bumblebee spins its' wings
As a toy windmill goes berserk

In this place
My heart heaves
Desperate to join you

I come alone now
To this place
Just me and my shadow
Which grows shorter as a linger

I don't cry
Here in this place
But coming to and going from
Tears fill the sockets of my
sorrow

In this place
Where flowers droop at headrests
I sit on your blanket of grass
No flowers
Just unspoken words that
Clench my gut, jam my heart

Over there a Mrs De Cesare has
erected
A wooden bench in loving
memory
Still I sit on the wet grass
As close as possible

You have no wooden bench, no
flowers
The least I could do is give you
my tears
To keep the grass green

Perhaps when I've written your
words
I'll let you see my tears

August 2000

The Fox

Just 4 people away from you
Is a limp arrangement of
sunflowers

Amongst them
Standing tall
A Bird of Paradise
Its' erect orange petals,
foxes ears
Burnished red bud,
its snout

A sentry
Protecting that 4th person

August 2000

Bold & Beautiful

I stole a flower today
From the one beside you
It didn't belong there anyway,
blown by the wind
A gerbera it was
Just its upside-down head
On the sunken clay mound

I took this gerbera
And bit by bit scattered petals
over you
Crimson on green
A comforter of sorts

Then I stubbed out my cigarette
Started for home
To watch The Bold and the
Beautiful

In the cover of a gum
I stood on the hill
As yet another procession began
Practicalities came first
Opening of the boot
Collapsible chair for the most
grievous
I wanted it to be a white coffin
Like the minister's robes
Needed to know I wasn't alone
Needed another mother, a mute
stranger
To comfort me.

September 2000

Growth emerging
from the
bone compost
Spring

Elastic Absence

I spoke to your second Mum
today
The one who took you in
When I was bald from tearing
my hair out
You were 13 then

Yesterday was the 13th
Her birthday
87 she is now

We didn't mention you
Sometimes with special people
Your name doesn't have to be
said
For you are always the elastic
that binds

I think I'll take her freesias,
stocks and pansies
To put some colour back into her
life

By the way, my hair grew back
But I'd rather be bald

September 2000

Humanity's Humanness

Though ten months have passed
Still I stumble
Knees grazed, bleeding, scabbed
from
Dragging myself through those
one-liners
You lured me with
(fly fishing in an empty pool)

It cuts so deep
You only find the one soul-mate
I might be asleep in the morning
when you come

Who's to blame
We all are
Each and everyone of us

September 2000

Bait

Each day brings a new picture
As I step into the shower or fall
asleep, whatever

Today it's you at Parliament
Station
Disheveled, standing at the top
of the underground escalators
Searching the mob of workers
As they ascend from the
cavernous burrows

What colour is her hair this day?
Carrot? Streaks of purple?
Your promising Goddess full of
false promise
You search and search until told
to move on
Loitering isn't allowed
You reach for your wallet to
prove you're somebody
But it's on the pier where you
left it
Last night when your mates took
you fishing
With a slab and a bag of bait

Even with a pole, a tinny and
best friends
You couldn't stop the pacing of
your mind

One minute silhouetted by
the moon
The next, an emptiness
A precursor of what was to come

Wandering, searching, bleeding
for her
Sleeping in a laneway
Awake at sunrise for
She might catch the 6am rattler!
Instead it's you who hops a train
home

Your very last ride

September 2000

Everlasting

I saw your Nan today
Gave her a bunch of everlasting
daisies
She'll probably stick them in a
vase
Leave them there till she's carted
away

I couldn't go into the backyard
Used the front door instead
We sat in the kitchen
Beside the wood stove
Where she cradled you in Winter
All those years ago

Talked about everything but you,
until
How are you handling your
grief?

A bit easier, she said
That photo you gave me
When I go to bed, it's the last
thing I see
The way you captured his
expression
Head on an angle, cheeky grin,
'Night Nan'.
Then she went back to talking
about safe things

Later, sitting on the stained toilet
I made myself stare out the
cracked window
To the corner of the yard
At the seemingly innocuous
bottlebrush
Where you frantically
tap-danced mid-air

Beneath the bottlebrush she's
planted blue hyacinths

A bit like everlasting daisies
really, hyacinths

September 2000

Janis Tait

Dry Storms

Often now
A storm
Gathers behind my eyes
And if I don't blink
But stare straight ahead
Like a sightless woman
The storm fills my head
And I have to gulp, gulp
So tears won't flood me

September 2000

Then

In my Father's day…
He had to wind up the
gramophone
Whereas now we slot in a disc

In my mother's day…
She wore rags between her legs
And now an assembly line spits
out sanitised plugs

In my day…
Death was like a fiction
Unlike today

September 2000

Stillness

When I woke this morning
There was a stillness
A holding of breath sort of
stillness
And not because
For only the fifth time in 30 years
There's to be a full moon tonight
on Friday 13th

More of a stillness
Because me, myself, have
reached a grief stage
Where I've become a distillery
of sorts
Melted emotions
Simmering
Waiting to be bottled

October 2000

Waiting

The anniversary must be soon,
they say
With soft smiles, eyes downcast

I start to panic
What is expected of me?
A torrent of tears
So swift I'll come adrift?
Fists flailing at the Wailing Wall?
Or even
That a mute grief sends me
screaming?

If I do none of these things
Will they think heartless,
no-good mother?
Or will they silently watch
Sure that if not this anniversary
Then the next

October 2000

Empty Seabed

Some crustaceans lay their eggs
And they wait these eggs
Sometimes for ten years
Wait for a cyclone to swirl
and toss
Just the right nutrients onto the
seabed
And the eggs grow
Hatch

I am the crustacean
You my egg
And you waited for the time
When you could release yourself
From the empty seabed

October 2000

Ambushed

I see that
A war rages over there
And an 8-year-old is shot dead

I read that
Here, in this city
Random murders take place
daily

And I hear that
The elderly are duped out of life
savings

I feel
Nothing
Though I utter sympathy

It's hard to feel
When an inner war rages
Unabated
Depleting my ammunition
Random bullets
Puncturing those unseen
parts

Thank God for camouflage!
For they'd turn away at the
destruction

The pot-holed ricochets of
hissing grief
Make me gasp for air

Living Death

Determined not to end up
Flat
Like a tyre

October 2000

Running on Empty

Hidden feelings
Well-hidden
'Coping' was the operative word
Coping
Not unlike copying

Aping a previous existence
Of a smile and curtsey
While you somehow coped
Had to

For on the other side of coping
Survival wasn't an option

October 2000

You, in Nature

Leaves falling

I catch them
These dried offerings

Leaves falling

Loose skin from limbs
Shedding colours
Too beautiful for death

Leaves falling

I catch them
Over and over

Press them between pages
Never to be opened

October 2000

Stolen by Stealth

A policeman at my door
Seems a robbery across the road
A break-I
Do I know anything?
Seen anything?
Throw some light on it?

No, but there's been a thief in my
house
He came during the night
Robbed us of our most precious

He'd been planning for weeks,
months even
While all the time
We'd been planning our
existence

I knew nothing
Saw nothing
Too busy

This stealthy thief
Crept in through the cracks of
Love and self-worth
Took up residence in my Son's
mind
Ate away at the laneways and
backroads
Until it came to the crossroad

And there it smugly sat
Biding its time
Only speaking when he dared to
vacillate
Blaming, egging him on
Deluding him into taking that
road
Away from the junction

No, officer, I haven't made a
claim
It wasn't that the premium
would increase
More that, I'm still trying to
work out
The cost to us all

October 2000

Remembrance

Darkness invades my head
And a tidal wave slams at my
stomach
All the while I think of you

I'm a sponge
Waiting for the time
When the excesses of grief
Are squeezed from my body

But this will never happen
As all the while I think of you

The frightening fog in my head
Clears slightly
Only when I have to focus on
Going from A to B
Doing 1,2, 3

All the while I think of you
This burning grief devours
Leaving my heart in ashes
Imprisoning memories, feelings
That no longer have anywhere
to go

Today, tears roll out
Stinging, as if in self-flagellation
I lie on my bed
See the sun still shines
While the cat miaows and the
potatoes burn

And I want to leave all of this
To go in search of you
To just stand beside you
My towering Son
Just for a minute
Please, just for a minute

And if I could see that
You were safe
And that a constant warmth
embraced you
I would gladly return to all this

And if not?
If you were scared, shivering
Well then, I'd stay with you
And start at the beginning
When there was just you and I

Till then,
I'll scoop up the ashes of my
heart
All the while I think of you

October 2000

The Illusion of Rhythms

What do you see from that
distance?
North, south, east and west
From which direction do
you see?

Now that you are distanced
Do you see the whole picture
Or just random shots that
Leave questions unanswered
Needs not met?

Do you see me from that
distance?
The way I automatically surface
when the alarm goes off
How I religiously serve decent
meals at regular times
Even the way I attack weeds on a
given day

Rhythms can be deceitful
Hiding subterranean currents
That do the most damage

October 2000

The Ties that Bind

When you were in that black
hole
Did you know what you were
doing
When you let that halo slip into a
noose
Leaving your neck scored,
equator like?

You couldn't have fathomed how
Forever after I relive that
moment
When I tie my dressing gown
Pull the cord on a rubbish bag
Fasten my watchband
Even putting on a necklace
Illuminates your last moments
Scores into my every cell
The depth of that blackness

October 2000

Simplicity/Pattern No. 1

They say life's a pattern
Cross-stitch and drop stitch
An integral part of the moss
stitch

As you were born your template
was made
By the lasso around your neck

Entering the world blue
Leaving the same way

October 2000

Torture

I should have kicked your
teeth in
Ripped your eyes out
Burnt matches under your nails
Then given you a Chinese Burn

Not to punish you
But to make you
Feel
Enough to stay

November 2000

The Gift

Paper, silver, gold, rubies
What shall I give you for this
Our 1st Anniversary?

The ashes that were my heart?

Sapphires, Emeralds, Diamonds,
Opals
There aren't enough gems for
anniversaries
That reach into eternity

(though you did score an eternity
ring around your neck)

November 2000

Anniversary Cusp

Near midnight
And I teeter
On the cusp of
The day you lived
And
The day you died

A year since you left us numbed
by grief
Angry, too, that you let death
beckon
Crook its dirty finger
Promising you what?

A soothing sleep
Nestled forever in a valley green
Even relief for those left behind?

I fucking taught you about
stranger danger!
And Death is the most dangerous
stranger of all!

November 2000

The First

Your cuppa's ready, he shouts
from the kitchen
We're coming, I call as I close
my journal

And though only I walk down
the hall
(the words about you clutched to
my chest)
I think nothing odd about
answering WE instead of I
For wherever I go you are
with me
Weighing me with your death
Elevating my spirit for having
known you

The sweet tea tastes sour
As I remember on this Remembrance Day
How at this exact hour I arrived
home
After identifying you as my son,
my lost son
Waking your brothers to tell
them of their greatest loss
The way my youngest woke,
befuddled,
(his 'No…Nos' still echo in
my head)
how he turned his face to the
wall as if to shut out the truth

And my middle son,
His look of horror and, yes,
expectancy

I have no memory of ringing
family and friends
Doorbell incessantly chimed as
Bouquets and arrangements
arrived
Florists looking downcast at
Bright flowers screaming a
celebration

Then people milling, touching
when words failed
Anger, blame, hovering too close
Fear striking out at other parents
That this could be contagious

The Grievers preferring the
backyard
The sun illuminating tears
Stooped shoulders
And weeds
A becalming warmth
Deluding me into denying
I was forever beached

The phone…and it's your friend
Wanting to know how I'm, we're
all coping
On this Remembrance Day
Are we all in bed still?

I tell him my husband's cleaning
the shower
And my son's hanging out the
washing
That they'll do anything for me
On this Day of Days

I try to keep my promise to you
And as I do
Fingers slide over tears
Falling onto the keyboard

asd J uil A nnn S ;;; O eiuuuuuu-
uuuuuu N

I failed the test of saving you
Can I pass this test?

11th November 2000

218

Dried Petals

I made the pilgrimage today
With scrubbing brush and bucket
And a red rose that had no
fragrance

The rain had beaten me to it
Washing clay off the words
That now seem so trite
No-one had beaten me to
the vase
I filled with the beautiful
hybrid rose

Some people have a Friendship
Garden
Where they plant cuttings from
friends

I have a Remembrance Garden
In which I dig over memories
Gather fallen petals
A pot-pourri to cover you
When I make the pilgrimage

11th November 200

Invisible Weight

Life, death, regret
12 months to the day yesterday
When I relived all of these
emotions
That have loaded me down
Like Simpson's Donkey
The other 364 days of the year

Yesterday, Simpson overloaded
me
Buckling my knees
As I struggled to walk the
distance
Life clinging to a stirrup
Death hanging on grimly
Regret astride in the saddle

At the end of the trail
Simpson kicked Death aside
Tenderly carried Life to the Tent
of Hope

I waited
All the dark night I waited
For Simpson to take the dreadful
load from the saddle

When the sun rose
And my back was concave
I looked but there was nothing
to see

But the weight,
Oh, the weight

12th November 2000

Janis Tait

Dry Season

So much I write about my river
of tears
Bemoaning it will never run its
course

Tonight on the telly
I watched a man crying
Really crying
As he put a gun to his head

And I wondered about your
tears
In those final moments
Did they pour profusely?
Or just slide slowly?

No, I think you didn't cry
Couldn't have
For if you had
You'd still be with me

November 2000

Sharp Edged Bluntness

Though I'm clawing my way
back
From the blackness of the
anniversary
Your death's still sharp
For me
For everyone
Though some seem blunted by it
Me too, sometimes

Blunt is when I think I should
feel more
Sharp is when I can feel no more

November 2000

The Gamut

There are moments in life when
we are dead
But that's better than being dead
forever

So, too, there are times
When we nearly burst with joy

Conversely, torrential tears drain
us of desires

But always
Always
Always
Always

A pervading glimmer of light
Re-souls our faith in humanity

Well…nearly always

November 2000

4:30am

More coffee, black forest cake?
I entice, bribe them
Dreading their going
For when they do
I'm left to again wade through a
reality
That doesn't include you.

Sultry, steaming, sweating tears of Summer

You'd have enjoyed my 50th
Wine, especially the beer
You could've snuck around the
sideway with me
Shared a reefer under a sky
studded with diamantés
That became even more
luminous with each drag
You could have giggled at the
antics of the Oldies
As they laughed at their own
jokes
And farted uncontrollably
As alcohol freed them up
Then your brother loosely
laughing
At my indiscreet fart
As I laughed at FF's anecdote
Of how her car mounted the
letterbox
(Did the letterbox enjoy it!)
Even funnier...
The spa motor overheating
Burning undies & bras strung on

the line
Wine bloodying the carpet and
velvet chair
Heat stains on my prized
mahogany table
Laundry door off its hinges

Yes, you could be sitting here
Watching
As I scribble words

All of these things
And more
You could have done
If that insidious snake
Hadn't wriggled into your head
Making you strike out at yourself

More coffee?
Black forest cake?
Anyone?

17th December 2000

Eternal Eclipse

If I was a turtle
Only now would my head
Emerge from my shell
Tentatively blinking
At the sun's harshness
That illuminates reasons for
happiness

Yet exposes the blackness of grief

18th December 2000

Janis Tait

1970-1999

Dates
The yardstick of existence
1970-1999
the dash between your coming
and going
So symbolic of your journey
For your were always on the go
As you tried to tango your
demons
Off the dance floor

There'll be no dash for me to
mark my journey
Instead,
Exclamation marks
As I rumba to a tune only I can
hear

If only you'd added your name
to my Dance Card
Together we could have invented
a new dance

Perhaps.

18th December 2000

Warning!

Do not allow grief to enter
Do not open the door to a
presence that
Gnaws and gnaws and gnaws
until
You become who you aren't

No, you do not allow grief to
enter

Unbidden, it slips beneath
eyelids
That dark dream
Inwardly worming its way to the
Soft centre of Marzipan Death

And when you break in half
They will see the heart rot;
The putrefaction of petrified love

No! Do not open the door for
you will
Surrender to the inevitability of
Recycled memories
That will lurch
Against your walls
Shredding an already torn spirit

22nd December 2000

Jewish Heaven

Up there
Where there's no oxygen
Do you celebrate Christmas?
Does humble Jesus want mass
acknowledgement?

Or don't you celebrate this
festivity?

Probably not

For if you did
Easter would be compulsory
And that'd sort of give you
false hope

You know, the Resurrection
and all

23rd December 2000

Merry Christmas

Have you been promoted yet?
Or are you still in Limbo?

I know what Limbo is

It's that place of isolation
Where others can't reach
Not until forgiveness settles like
dandruff
Unable to be shrugged off

It's a dislocated island
Unreachable by warmth
Where pieces of me are scattered
Cowpats, solidified by guilt

23rd December 2000

New Year

When the sky rockets soar to
nowhere
And the catherine-wheels run
out of spin
I'll gather myself together
Cross hands and start to sing

It's me who'll sing the loudest
As if I've just begun!
But I'll be drowning out the
sound
Of that bereavement clock within

31st December 2000

Would it?

Would it have made any
difference
If you'd been conceived
On an inner-spring mattress
Instead of a dusty vinyl seat
In a grey ute?

That they hadn't made me close
my legs
Leaving you to gag in my
mucous
And when the doctor arrived
and parted my legs
You dived into the air
Stilled from the anchor that
hugged your blue neck

Would it have made any
difference
If I'd held you
Those ten days they imprisoned
you
In that glass box
Pure air pumping in a chest
struggling to rise

Second-hand milk wouldn't have
helped much, either
(a solitary existence, a tin cup
and hand pump)
"Here's your baby", the nurse
said

as she handed the real thing to
other mothers
Not for me the sucking of lips on
yearning nipples
But the squish, squelch of rubber
that drained me of
Nurture
The clanking of tin against the
glass phial that held me to
ransom against
Fulfillment

And when finally I banshee
wailed at my emptiness
She came running
Steered by the black habit that
sailed behind
And she wheeled me to the huge
glassed room
Where they held you prisoner

There you were
Pink
And
Beautiful
And I stroked you
Stroked you through the
glass door
Only wide enough to fit my hand
Stroked you and stroked you
until
"Time's up", said the moored sail

I had to leave you there where

Jesus hung and Mary smiled
And go back to the sterile flat
with empty cot

In a relentless heat-wave, twice a
day I hailed the No. 5
Clutching the still-warm milk as
if a grenade
Bounding along in a bus that
stopped at the wooden cross
That bore no resemblance to my
suffering

Forever you gulped, guzzled my
white tears through the glass
opening
Until one day they said I could

Open the lid

I lifted you out
Gingerly held you
Waited for this flood of bonding
But it was love that swamped me
And it was me now that couldn't
get my breath
I was a virgin being deflowered
by the force of love
And I could grapple, understand
how

Mary was a virgin until she had
Jesus

At home you cried all night,
every night
I resorted to treacle on your
dummy
Kept a tin of it by my bed
One morning I woke to find you
deep-sleeping
The dummy stuck to your eyelid
That in the middle of the night
I'd thought was your mouth

Would it have made any
difference?

December 2000

Epiphany

I took down the decorations
today
The ones hung just weeks ago
And I thought how you did just
that
Hung yourself some 60 weeks
ago

Did you understand?

Truly understand how you were
Knotting the roots of your family
tree
Making tomorrow never

Did you stop to think?

So easily snuffing generations
of hope
A past made redundant

In the dead of night you stole
2? 3? 4?, less grandchildren
To shade me in old age

Tomorrow's never now

December 2000

A real tale

Once upon a time
A long time ago
When I was grieving
Really grieving
That deep, deep grieving
That if you're lucky only visits;
My ovaries died in sympathy

Now that deep grief visits again
My breast has gone out in
sympathy
A lump of resentment has
gathered

Appropriate really
Considering you're my sorrow
You were nurtured at that breast
Suckled and burped till you
dropped off to sleep

And now that great soother's
become puckered and lumpy
Might even drop me off to sleep

No-one's the wiser that I'm
disintegrating
They weren't when I suffered my
biggest
Amputation
No prosthesis will ever fit

Once upon a time there was
Janis

January 2001

Never-ending Clock

I breathe at your memory

Sigh at my loss

Gasp at the emptiness

Then I go back to breathing

Because

Someone keeps winding the
crazy clock

25th January 2001

Janis Tait

Excavate

This gnawing inside me
Eats a canyon so deep
No amount of fill
Will replenish

This gnawing inside me

What if it stops?

Then to keep on feeling
Something, anything
I'll have to cannibalize
Myself
To survive
This gnawing inside me

26th January 2001

The Diver

When I mention you
There is silence
Embarrassed…pitying…
I don't know what to say silence

Don't they understand
That if I don't tell my memories
I'll go mad
By saying your name
I dredge the wonderful,
foolhardy, inane, funny, weird
things
You said and did
The springboard from which I
dive
Hold my breath
Surfacing only when I'm
replenished
By the fact of you

26th January 2001

Overtime

Weak and yellow like a
jaundiced baby
The old man is dying

I'm impatient with his whining
and crying

Greedy old man

Still, I rub his arm and tell him

Don't be afraid,
It's time to rest,
You've had a long life,
Go gently

Still he rails at death

Talk to him about dying, I say
To the old man's good wife
Who now carries a hanky with
her broom
Don't avoid it
He knows

I do, I do, she says
Sweeping and blowing
I tell him we are not all born at
the same time
And so we can't go together
And that he has to go to make
room for the young

Does that mean your early death
My son
Gave him overtime?

26th January 2001

Limitless

An old diary unearthed…
In childish scrawl
A tattered jewel on a page

Aftermath
Forever…

I love

You

Mum

500

Now in a pewter frame
It sits by my bed
As re-enforcement

26th January 2001

Collectable Junk

I threw out junk today
Useless things like

Schoolbooks

Plastic skittles

Punctured footballs

I didn't throw out your fishing
seat
Collapsible, like you

18th February 2001

Ghost Writing

Odd that I'm the best recycler
around
(kitchen scraps, shredded
newspaper, ashes
all go into the black hole)
And yet, though desperate to
keep you
If only on paper
I refuse to recycle words
Already written

If only I could have the intimate
immediacy
Of reaching you this way

Forever

But you were a man of few
words
You wouldn't want me
To overwrite

18th February 2001.

Belated

I rail at the thought
You might be forgotten
Castigating those who look away
At the mention of your name

And yet...and yet...

This week
I forgot
Your birthday
Remembered
A day later
And I don't know whether my
swamping
Stems from guilt
Or the mere fact
You would have been 31

23rd February 2001

Not Yet, Not Yet

After they lowered you into the
ground
I dropped green apricots
From your tree
Onto mahogany shining
Like great-gran's piano lid

And like those apricots
I began to wither that day
Intestines knotting
Senseless feelings
A reactor shutting down

The time nears
I will say goodbye
No, not to you
Never

When you left
I became a caterpillar
My cocoon a shroud

The time nears
I will say goodbye to

Guilt

Self Pity

and

Regret

Each day the cocoon
Strains to hold these feelings

I will not leave you behind
But take you with me on my
flight
And with each wing flutter
My heart too will soar:
My unrelenting passion

The time nears
But not yet
Not yet

26th February 2001

Moving House

These are the thing we gathered:

Pack of ABC play cards
Cricket hat
Walkman
Drum Tobacco and matches
Cold stubbie
My favourite earring
And my letter to you

Symbolic gifts we surrounded
you with

We had to open the lid again
Your brother added a pack of
tobacco papers
Something I'd forgotten

March 2001

235

Janis Tait

Goodnight Kisses

I want you back
Rigid in the leather chair
Pretending to shrug off
The kisses
I planted
When I said goodnight

March 2001

Crumbling Stairs

I dream of ladders
Borrowing, hiring extensions
To reach you

When I enter the blackness
Stars my streetlights,
Rungs begin to disintegrate

I climb and climb
Like a childhood dream
Where I ran in the same place
So afraid of what was behind me

Was it like that for you?
Running on the spot
Until the fear caught up

March 2001

Past, Present, Future

A fruit box
That's what your treasures filled
When I was able to clear out
your room

Birthday / Get Well / Xmas cards
In a battered wallet, your
business card
Man of Action
And a meticulously folded
newspaper article,
'Make Marijuana Legal'
with a photo of the Opposition
Leader
who wanted to do just that
Magazines on Cricket and Top
Fishing Ideas
Binoculars
Turners Four Figure
Mathematical Tables
Very Best of Crowded House
Comics
Application to join the Labor
Party
Cash tin – lock forced
Special ring that protected you
from evil
Fishing hooks
Dog-eared photo album I'd put
together
Your only addition,

Polaroid snaps of 2 marijuana
plants
(seedlings to maturity)

I couldn't pack your love away
It wouldn't have fitted in the box
marked
"Yellow Cling Peaches"

March 2001

237

Janis Tait

Façade

Tonight
Unlike you
I'm unable to sleep

Today was nothing out of the
ordinary

As the paddocks whizzed past
I laughed, chatted, stared
Then did the same at my father's

No, nothing out of the ordinary

As behind the mask I slipped
and dipped
To that place
Where reality waits
As sure as my unmarked
tombstone

Waits
Demanding surrender
To the simple pain
Of losing you

March 2001

It

Some days It bangs against me
Others, Its prickle
Reminds me that
Never again shall I feel nothing

Some days It sits in my gut
Like a rotten egg
Others, It travels arterial
highways and laneways
Hitting dead ends

On any given day It just is
Reaching into every pumping
organ
Trying to shut me down

If It had a voice; It would bellow
Feelings; a burning bruise
Colour; blackest of black
Age; forever

Forever bellowing a big black
bruise of despair

Some days, though, the round-
abouts and humps
Still Its progress
Others, It escapes, surging
arterial rivers
Until It reaches the heart-lake

When that happens
The overspill floats me
Closer to you

March 2001

Living Death

Branded

I don't need to be told
That life is precious

Though, too often I'm reminded
When the Black Prod of Death
Sears
Buckling me from the heat

March 2001

Dreaded Cobwebs

How are you coping?

I just keep running

Careful you don't wear out your
shoes

More like my soul

Once I used to enjoy my
company
Now…

There's a deathly quiet in
solitude
That seeps into my soul
Leaving me bereft
A cobweb of dread
That invisibly clutches

And so I must keep running

8th March 2001

Echoes

It's been so dry
Even the weeds have carked it

I miss the rain
Soothing drops of comfort
A cover for my tears

You liked the rain, too
No raincoat or prissy umbrella
for you
Instead, baring yourself to the
Accompanying symphony of the
storm
That must have echoed
The zigzagging tremors in
your mind

An echo that made you not
so alone.

8th March 2001

Rhythms

I noticed the humming
When the cat purred on my lap
Humming that took me to a
place
I haven't visited
Since you left

A simple place of
Feelings harmonious
Where hope stirs
Tickling my senses

And so the time has come
The scabs of my sorrow are dry
Though always, always
A corner of my heart will bleed
for you,
My Son

The time has come

14th April 2001